Sending Your Government a Message

E-mail Communication Between Citizens and Government

C. Richard Neu • Robert H. Anderson • Tora K. Bikson

Supported by the John and Mary R. Markle Foundation

RAND
Science and Technology

The research described in this report was supported by the John and Mary R. Markle Foundation under Grant No. G96328.

Library of Congress Cataloging-in-Publication Data

Neu, C. R. (Carl Richard), 1949- .
    Sending your government a message : e-mail communication
between citizens and government / C. Richard Neu, Robert H.
Anderson, Tora K. Bikson.
      p. cm.
    " Prepared for the John and Mary R. Markle Foundation by
RAND's Science and Technology Institute."
    " MR-1095-MF."
    Includes bibliographical references.
    ISBN 0-8330-2754-9
    1. Administrative agencies—United States—Communication
systems. 2. Executive departments—United
States—Communication systems. 3. Electronic mail
systems—United States. I. Anderson, Robert H. (Robert Helms),
1939- . II. Bikson, Tora K. , 1940- . III. Title.
JK468.T4N48   1999
384.3 ' 4—dc21   99-37564
                                              CIP

Published 1999 by RAND
1700 Main Street, P.O. Box 2138, Santa Monica, CA 90407-2138
1333 H St., N.W., Washington, D.C. 20005-4707
RAND URL: http://www.rand.org/
To order RAND documents or to obtain additional information,
contact Distribution Services: Telephone: (310) 451-7002;
Fax: (310) 451-6915; Internet: order@rand.org

In 1995, RAND published a report exploring the feasibility and societal implications of providing "universal" access to electronic mail within the United States (Robert H. Anderson et al., *Universal Access to E-Mail: Feasibility and Societal Implications*, MR-650-MF). Among the nine policy conclusions and recommendations in that report were these:

- It is critical that electronic mail be a basic service in a National Information Infrastructure;

- It is important to reduce the increasing gaps in access to basic electronic information services, specifically, access to electronic mail services;

- There are no fundamental technical barriers to providing universal access to electronic mail services.

The sponsor of that study, the John and Mary R. Markle Foundation, supported a subsequent study on a related subject, which has resulted in the current report. The question motivating this second study was: What are the opportunities for and the obstacles to increased use of the Internet and electronic mail to facilitate communication between government agencies and their citizen clients?

Of particular interest are interactions between government agencies and *individual* citizens—not downloading tax forms at a kiosk or public library computer, but interactions involving personal information, iterated communications between an individual and a government agency, and use of a personal electronic mailbox for the individual.

This report explores this possibility for expanded citizen-government personalized electronic communication. It provides an informal survey of current state uses of such communication, supplemented by two more substantial case studies of potential use. It also uses 1997 Current Population Survey data to update the electronic access trends in the United States that were highlighted in the 1995 study.

This report should be of interest to government agencies interested in providing services to citizens via electronic communication, to organizations and individuals interested in expanding on-line usage to those currently without such access, and to policymakers attempting to understand and shape—or at least ameliorate—the social impacts of the continuing information revolution.

This study was performed under the auspices of RAND's Science and Technology research unit, which is directed by Stephen Rattien. For further information on this study, please contact the authors:

CR_Neu@rand.org
Tora_Bikson@rand.org
Robert_Anderson@rand.org

CONTENTS

FIGURES

TABLES

SUMMARY

The reader of this report has most likely bought a book from Amazon.com or perhaps even participated in an eBay.com on-line auction—two electronic transactions on the Internet involving contractual obligations, goods, and services. He or she has probably *not* conducted a similar two-way electronic interaction (e.g., involving licenses, taxes, or other substantive transactions) with a local, state, or federal government agency.

Certain questions arise: Why are millions of dollars' worth of interactive transactions taking place daily on the Internet, yet important (legal, monetary, etc.) on-line transactions between government and citizen are not? Why do we assume the reader of this report (presumably college educated, probably with a family income at or above average for the United States) has access to the Internet, even though nearly half the U.S. population does not?

This report considers such questions on the way to addressing a somewhat more pointed and immediate question: What roles can or should electronic mail (e-mail) and the Internet play in facilitating communication between government agencies and their citizen clients? It also addresses an important subsidiary question: What role should government agencies have in encouraging the spread of Internet and e-mail access?

We are concerned here not with bulk, "wholesale" applications, such as providing downloadable tax forms or agency brochures. Useful as those services are, we are concerned with personalized, "retail" communications—i.e., those initiated either by a citizen or the government, addressed to or from the individual, and containing information specific to that individual. For simplicity, we refer to these communications as "e-mail," although they may well be initiated by interactions with a World Wide Web fill-in-the-blanks form or similar means.

An earlier report (Anderson et al., 1995), which was co-authored by two of the present authors, studied prospects for universal access to e-mail. We continue that study here by focusing on prospects for government-citizen electronic interactions that might make government services cheaper or more effective and that, in the process, might encourage more of the population to become "wired." We survey examples of current government use of e-mail for interactive provision of services. We then examine in more depth two case studies of potential government use of "retail" government-citizen interactions, both of which are high volume and touch disparate and diverse portions of our society: the Health Care Financing Administration's interactions with citizens regarding Medicare benefits, and California's Employment Development Department's handling of unemployment insurance claims. In each case, we seek advantages—both to citizens and to government operations—from the use of e-mail and consider risks, barriers, and challenges in providing on-line, interactive access.

THE MEDIUM AND THE MESSAGES: CURRENT GOVERNMENT USE

Given the diversity of electronic means of communication, some clarification of terminology is important. We distinguish two message types: *form based* and *free form*. Form-based, or structured, messages rely for their formulation on prestructured response fields—for instance, by permitting only responses that are selected from a menu of choices or by accepting only a limited range of answers. Free-form messages, in contrast, have contents (outside of the message header) that are open ended and not formally prestructured. The distinction is significant because it indicates the extent to which messages are susceptible to automated processing, or to handling by means of rules and software agents with access to a database.

We also distinguish messages as *simple* or *complex*. Simple messages attempt only to convey information. Complex ones try to accomplish some action, such as applying for a business license. This distinction carries implications regarding system costs, data requirements, and security concerns that entail special technical features or raise differing implementation concerns.

Features of Complex, Form-Based Messages

We sought examples of complex messages in government-citizen interactions. The majority we found were form based. Other useful categorizations of complex on-line interactions are

- *Financial vs. other official transactions.*

- *Directionality, history, and interactivity* (who initiates the dialog, the extent to which it relies on a stored history of the individual, and whether the interactivity is real-time or not).

- *Iterations, asynchronous responses, and out-of-band components* (whether the interactions are iterated or one-shot, whether they are asynchronous or not, and whether out-of-band auxiliary communication—such as using postal mail to send a password— is necessary).

Survey of Official State Uses of E-Mail

We sent an e-mail survey to chief information officers in all 50 states. At the time of the survey (summer 1997), only a small number of states had made real progress toward use of digital technologies for full official transactions with citizens. Our general findings from this survey are that

- Almost all states post forms, including most tax forms, for downloading. A sizable number of states allow electronic tax filing, but only through a trusted third-party intermediary.

- State Web servers typically communicate electronically with thousands of people every day, peaking at tax season as citizens download needed tax forms and instructions. (These are simple transactions in our rubric.)

- No states were offering citizens the opportunity to make their applications for social welfare benefits on-line in 1997.

Barriers to Increased Electronic Communications

Based on our survey, the main barriers to increased use of complex electronic communications are security, costs, and socially constructed barriers such as technophobia and (dis)trust.

We conclude from our informal survey that, first, there is no "one size fits all" solution to the disparate communications needed between government and citizens. Second, laws and regulations will need to change to assure the official status of these communications, especially with relationship to certain concepts, such as "signature" and "original document," that are strewn throughout state and federal public law. Third, many of the practical problems in the use of digital media for official interactions are being addressed by the research community, such as through the National Science Foundation's new "digital government" research initiative.

Case Study: Health Care Financing Administration and the Medicare Program

Some 38 million Americans are enrolled in the Medicare program, which is administered by the Health Care Financing Administration (HCFA) within the Social Security Administration. During 1997, about 846 million claims were filed under this program. *Claims* for Medicare benefits are submitted by health-care providers, such as hospitals, nursing homes, and physicians. Well over 80 percent of such claims are today filed electronically. In addition, a large number of communications are carried out directly with beneficiaries (individual citizens). These personalized communications, the vast majority of which are *not* electronic, are in three categories: initial enrollment in the Medicare program, ad hoc customer service, and notices of claims processed.

Of the three types of communication between HCFA and individuals, the vast majority—and therefore those of greatest interest to our study—are notices sent by Medicare contractors informing beneficiaries that particular claims have been processed and explaining what part of the total bill will be paid by Medicare and what remains the responsibility of the beneficiary. Recent law[1] and revisions to reporting being implemented by HCFA will require approximately 300 million Medicare Summary Notices to be mailed each month. Needless to say, if a significant fraction of these could be handled electronically, the cost savings alone could be substantial. Web-based forms for interactions with beneficiaries could be processed automatically because of their form-based content, and there would be auxiliary advantages to beneficiaries such as form accessibility from a variety of locales and the option to provide information in a choice of languages.

A major initiative to consolidate all claims processing in two regional centers (with a third as backup) has recently been abandoned by HCFA. That "Medicare Transaction System" development would have provided central data hubs to support e-mail transmission of Medicare Summary Notices and perhaps e-mail-based customer service. Without this consolidation, the move to greater use of e-mail will have to proceed piecemeal and be negotiated with each of Medicare's more than 70 contractors.

Other barriers to e-mail use are beneficiary acceptance, the problem of security, and providing constancy in e-mail addresses so they do not change whenever a customer changes to a different Internet service provider (ISP).

Given the above factors, the highest priority for HCFA may be to cooperate with other government agencies to develop a mechanism for secure and reliable delivery of Medicare Summary Notices by e-mail. Other communications, such as providing customer support electronically, might best be postponed until a more robust infrastructure for truly secure two-way communication and for verifying the identity of e-mail correspondents is established.

---

[1]The Health Insurance Portability and Accountability Act of 1996 (P.L. 104-191), also known as the Kennedy-Kassebaum Act.

Case Study: California's Employment Development Department and Its Unemployment Insurance Program

California's Employment Development Department (EDD) administers the state's unemployment insurance (UI), job service, employment tax, and disability insurance programs. In California today, over 28 million claims of varying types are filed annually for UI benefits.

Individualized interactions associated with the UI claims process typically are as follows:

1. Claimant obtains and completes an initial claim form and turns it in at an EDD field office.

2. Claimant is interviewed by field office staff to determine eligibility. If a routine monetary determination can be made, field office staff enter data into a centralized UI database.

3. If the initial claim form is complete and correct but questions remain that field office staff cannot resolve (e.g., about eligibility), a determination is made based on a telephone interview with an adjudication staff member.

4. Successful claimants are sent a continued claim form to complete and return by mail.

5. When returned, the continued claim form is scanned by optical character recognition machines at one of two state claims centers; claimant is sent a new form that must be filed two weeks later to maintain eligibility.

6. Questions that arise are handled by customer service representatives.

At present, EDD provides no mechanisms for Internet-based retail communication between the UI program and its clients. EDD relies extensively on telephone-based systems for answering client questions via automated interactive voice response units.

The area of initial UI claims filing (step 1, above) has significant potential for savings. Both EDD staff time and costs could be cut if e-mail filing could replace current procedures in a nonnegligible number of cases. (Of such claims, 90 percent are routine, and 60 to 70 percent involve repeat clients who are familiar with the processes and for which much requisite information is already on file.) Continued claims filing (step 5, above), which accounted for 23,625,000 individualized interactions in 1996, is another area ripe for possible e-mail use, since most of the processing is routine.

We do not foresee significant technology constraints to implementing e-mail procedures within the EDD. The primary constraints are security challenges and such "user equity" issues as system accessibility for all California residents.

Security and Related Technical Issues

A consistent theme running through our survey of state applications and two case studies is the need for secure communications. Not all communications between government agencies and citizens require a high level of security, but some do. The four main elements of secure communications are *authentication* (of sender and receiver), *data integrity* (the data are unchanged from source to destination), *nonrepudiation* (evidence is available to verify the integrity, origin, and receipt of the data), and *confidentiality* (information can be read only by authorized entities).

Some of these elements of secure communication can be provided between the sender's and the recipient's computers by encryption schemes that come within commercial browsers and e-mail programs, such as the secure multipurpose Internet mail extensions (S-MIME) protocol for secure mail and the secure sockets layer (SSL) protocol. To achieve all the needed elements, however, many observers believe that a public key infrastructure (PKI) is required. A PKI relies on "certificate authorities" (CAs) that issue digital certificates representing the identity of the user or granting the user various authorities (e.g., to access or modify certain information). They (or other institutions within the PKI system) must maintain certificate revocation lists that can be queried as needed to assure that a digital certificate is still valid, and they must perform other service functions such as replacing lost or stolen certificates. Certificates bind a user to the public key portion of a public-private encryption key pair on which a PKI is based.

Widespread and versatile communications between government agencies and citizens will depend on a CA or group of CAs that can meet the following criteria:

- Highly reliable identification of agencies and users;

- Local presence (to provide periodic in-person interactions to verify identity of a person seeking a certificate);

- Extensive customer service (to handle service requirements, such as answering questions and restoring or replacing compromised certificates).

Entities that might perform CA services include specialist firms tailored to providing CA services, banks, health insurance providers or health maintenance organizations, the Social Security Administration, the U.S. Postal Service, and state departments of motor vehicles.

Perhaps the most reasonable solution is a variety of CAs, competing among themselves to provide services and working within a "web of trust" framework that allows the honoring of one CA's certificates by another (at varying levels of authority).

The Federal Public Key Infrastructure Steering Committee is currently wrestling with these issues. It is also developing a "Bridge" facility allowing separate PKI systems within the federal government to share certificates and trusted relationships.

Among the security-related issues to be resolved are

- Standards for the responsibilities of CAs.

- How to manage and protect private keys (e.g., while stored in a person's personal computer).

- The legal status of electronic transactions.

- Key escrow (will it be required? under what circumstances?).

- Reconciliation of multiple laws and standards.

- Who will pay (for the costs of a secure communication infrastructure)?

- Relations among CAs (how to build a "web of trust" among competing and differing CAs).

Other issues meriting attention are (1) the implications of the possible desirability of a "token" (such as a "smart card") to provide positive identification of a user, (2) the handling of digital archives and audit trails, (3) how to manage the expectations of users, and (4) the possible detrimental effects of "spamming" and junk mail.

We believe the above issues can be dealt with and that technical solutions are available. We suggest an implementation strategy based on the following precepts:

- An incremental, experimental approach is key.

- Citizens should be able to "opt in"—i.e., should not be required to use electronic systems and services.

- Out-of-band communication will continue to be important—for example, for verifying the identity of an individual.

- Success will depend on education and training.

Trends in Citizen Use of Computers and Connectivity

An important aspect of citizen-government communication is citizen access to computers and connectivity. As part of this study, we updated our earlier analysis of relevant access trends (Anderson et al., 1995) with recent statistics available from the October 1997 Current Population Survey conducted by the Bureau of the Census for the Bureau of Labor Statistics. The current analysis permits study of those groups able to benefit now from on-line access to government, as well as those groups in danger of being left behind and for which some type of intervention or incentive may be necessary.

The results of our most recent analysis are not encouraging. Comparing 1997 to 1993 data, we found that many gaps in the availability of a computer at home were major in both years and had *widened* in the four-year interval:[2]

_____

[2]In each case given, we list the group with greater availability first.

- Second, 3rd, and 4th vs. bottom income quartile;
- White vs. Hispanic and black race/ethnicity;
- Age group 20–39 vs. 60+;
- Urban vs. rural.

Similarly, many gaps in the use of network services (from home or at work, to connect to e-mail, bulletin boards, or work communications, etc.) *widened:*

- Top (4th) vs. bottom income quartile;
- College vs. high school and dropout education levels;
- White vs. Hispanic and black race/ethnicity;
- Age group 20–39 vs. 60+;
- Urban vs. rural.

At times, the results are dramatic. For example, in 1997, 75 percent of individuals in the upper income quartile had access to a computer at home, while only 15 percent of those in the bottom quartile did. When considering access to network services (at home, at work), the corresponding numbers were 45 and 7 percent.

Our study confirms that there remains a "digital divide" between those who do and do not have access to computers and communication technologies. These disparities have persisted in spite of the fact that the relevant technologies have decreased dramatically in price (relative to what they can do) and increased markedly in user friendliness. The types of incentives to electronic government-citizen online participation we studied may therefore be important as components of any strategy aimed at bringing network access to those currently deprived of it.

Observations and Recommendations

Based on our sample of state experiments with e-mail and our case studies, we believe there is a strong case to be made for government agencies whose work generates significant volumes of personalized communication to immediately begin developing the means to use e-mail as a supplement to the more traditional postal or telephonic channels. The main reasons are that

- E-mail can be cheaper than postal or telephone communication.
- E-mail can allow improved service.
- Increased government use of e-mail can encourage "wiredness" within U.S. society, especially for groups not currently on-line.
- Citizens will eventually insist on communication with government agencies by e-mail.

However, there are a number of operational concerns to be addressed and important preconditions to be met for successful exploitation of e-mail:

- *Security.* There appear to be no serious technical barriers to providing even high levels of security. For some high-volume government applications, some combination of PKIs run by public or private authorities, and with some levels of shared trust among them, are likely to be necessary.

- *Free-form e-mail.* E-mail that is free form—i.e., not in a standardized or predictable format—offers few advantages over telephone or traditional written communication. It is unlikely to be responded to quickly, especially if agencies receive considerable volumes of it.

- *Information architectures to support e-mail communication.* Exploiting the full potential of e-mail may require government agencies to make major investments in information systems, beyond what may be required just to handle e-mail traffic, because of the opportunities for automated processing that e-mail might provide.

- *Reaching the "unwired."* Access to the Internet and to e-mail today is concentrated among the young, the well educated, and the relatively well-to-do. Agencies must avoid the perception that they are offering special services only to elite groups and must focus attention on outreach to the currently unwired.

- *Expanding Internet access.* For the type of two-way interactive access we envision, simple access to a public-use terminal (e.g., in a library or community center) will not suffice. Citizens will need individual e-mail accounts and addresses. Messages must be stored on some server, and someone must bear the costs of providing and maintaining this server.

- *A default Internet service provider?* Some private firms already offer free e-mail access. (Their revenue derives from advertising.) Is there, then, a role for a publicly funded e-mail service—perhaps targeted at individuals or households satisfying some means test? At present, the case for publicly funded access to Internet services seems weak, on both policy and political grounds.

- *E-mail addresses for all: a new role for the Postal Service?* Access to electronic services by those currently not participating might be encouraged by creating a unique e-mail address (as opposed to an e-mail account) for every resident or organization in the United States. Directories of those addresses (with some provision for privacy) would be available on-line. Messages sent to a standardized address could be routed to an existing e-mail account (e.g., at the person's business or ISP) or printed and delivered via regular postal mail. The address would remain consistent even if the user chose to change his or her ISP. A hybrid system of this sort might be operated by the U.S. Postal Service or another national service provider.

Government's Role

Some modest actions by a few government agencies at the federal, state, and local levels can play a useful role in smoothing the path to increased use of e-mail in communication between governments and citizens. These actions may also generate spillover benefits for nongovernment users of e-mail and may advance the goal of near-universal access to e-mail. Helpful government initiatives include the following:

1. *Explore opportunities for personalized e-mail communication.* There are many operational questions to be resolved. By considering which of their functions might be facilitated by e-mail communication with individual citizens, and experimenting with e-mail in less-demanding situations, agencies can begin

preparing for the day when they will find it necessary to communicate via e-mail.

2. *Articulate security standards for government e-mail communication.* The few key agencies that deal in large volumes of sensitive communication should begin the process of debating and defining how much, and what kind of, security will be adequate for their purposes. A coordinating body for this discussion already exists in the Federal Public Key Infrastructure Steering Committee.

3. *Contribute credibility—and perhaps facilities—to an infrastructure for secure e-mail.* By contracting with purveyors of secure e-mail services and certifying that they meet stringent government standards, agencies may lend credibility to a decentralized and nongovernmental infrastructure for secure e-mail, thereby expanding the usefulness of Internet access for many other purposes.

4. *Create a legal environment supportive of secure e-mail.* Issues must be resolved related to allowable levels and types of encryption, standardized digital signatures, and privacy protection for e-mail. Some of the regulatory and legal framework that now protects U.S. postal mail must be enacted for and tailored to the electronic domain.

5. *Give special attention to the needs of the "unwired."* Governmental actions can encourage and support access for the "digitally disadvantaged." This might take the form of establishing public-use terminals, with some level of instruction and assistance for would-be users, in accessible locations. These initiatives would dovetail with the following one to provide a "home on-line" for all.

6. *Provide e-mail addresses for all.* A national system of e-mail addresses, perhaps tied to the ".us" Internet domain and coupled with a mail-forwarding service (electronically for those having an e-mail service provider, and in hardcopy form for others), could be a cost-effective approach to expanding communication options and encouraging all citizens to take advantage of the growing abundance of information and opportunities available on-line.

ACKNOWLEDGMENTS

We are grateful to Lloyd N. Morrisett, President of the Markle Foundation at the time this work was begun, and to Zoe Baird, his successor, for their support and counsel throughout this project.

Bruce C. Vladeck, Administrator of HCFA at the time this study was begun, generously gave us permission to pursue our case study of HCFA's communications with Medicare beneficiaries. Joyce Somsak and Megan Arts of the HCFA staff were instrumental in guiding us to the many other staff members who patiently and clearly explained the workings of the Medicare program and the vast flow of communications related to it. Staff members at ten HCFA contractors also shared with us their procedures for managing the Medicare program on a day-to-day basis. We are grateful to all of these.

At California EDD, our request to identify and explore areas of individualized communications for potential case study purposes met with a positive response from Josetta Bull, Deputy Director, Information Technology Branch, and Deborah Bronow, Assistant Deputy Director, Unemployment Insurance Division. They facilitated meetings and made contacts for us with appropriate individuals throughout the department. We are especially grateful to Talbott Smith, Chief of the Administrative, Workforce and Enterprise Solutions Section in the Information Systems Division, and to Gretchen Jung, then Chief of the Oversight, Data and Support Section of the Unemployment Insurance Division, for giving us considerable amounts of their time and attention, providing us with needed data and documentation, and helping us to schedule appointments with representatives of other units over numerous visits to EDD. We appreciate as well the cooperation of the many other EDD unit representatives without whose assistance we could not have completed the case study.

Staff at other government agencies also offered insights into the potential for greater use of e-mail and the potential pitfalls that lie along the way. Especially helpful were Leo Campbell of the United States Postal Service and John Sabo of the Social Security Administration.

Among our RAND colleagues, Joanna Heilbrunn provided invaluable assistance, collecting much of the information for the HCFA case study and interviewing HCFA contractors. Maria Sanchez did much of the basic work that led to our survey of current government use of e-mail and the Internet. Ashin Rastegar assisted with the analysis of access to e-mail.

Finally, we are indebted to Ingo Vogelsang of the Boston University Economics Department, Lee S. Sproull of the Boston University School of Management, and Norman G. Litell, Director of Corporate Risk Management at Visa U.S.A., Inc., for insightful and constructive reviews of early drafts of this report.

Any errors in fact or judgment that remain in this report despite the efforts of all those noted above are, of course, our responsibility.

BREVITIES

ANOVA	analysis of variance
ARU	automated response unit
ATM	automated teller machine
CA	certificate authority
CATI	computer-assisted telephone interviewing
CIO	chief information officer
CPS	Current Population Survey
CSR	customer-service representative
CSTB	Computer Science and Technology Board
DoD	Department of Defense
EDD	Employment Development Department
EDI	Electronic Data Interchange
EOMB	Explanation of Your Medicare Benefits
ETS	Educational Testing Service
HCFA	Health Care Financing Administration
IDS	Internet Demographic Study
IRS	Internal Revenue Service
ISP	Internet service provider
ITSC	Information Technology Support Center
IVR	interactive voice response

MPU	minutes-per-unit
MSN	Medicare Summary Notice
MTS	Medicare Transaction System
NACHA	National Automated Clearing House Association
NSF	National Science Foundation
OCR	optical character recognition
PC	personal computer
PEBES	Personal Earnings and Benefits Estimate Statement
PIN	personal identification number
PKE	public key encryption
PKI	public key infrastructure
S-MIME	secure multipurpose Internet mail extensions
SAGE	streamlined adjudication graphical environment
SSA	Social Security Administration
SSL	secure sockets layer
SSN	Social Security number
UI	Unemployment Insurance
USPS	United States Postal Service
WARN	Worker Adjustment and Retraining Notification

Chapter One

INTRODUCTION

Americans are changing the way they communicate. Recent years have seen the blossoming and the wide acceptance of new forms of networked digital communication. The most prominent of these new communication media, of course, are the Internet and the World Wide Web. In increasing numbers, Americans are turning first to the World Wide Web when they seek information on subjects ranging from current events to weather conditions in a distant city, from financial-market developments to local traffic congestion. Institutions and organizations of every stripe—schools and universities, hospitals, public-interest and advocacy groups, trade associations, dance companies and symphony orchestras, think tanks and philanthropic foundations—explain their missions, accomplishments, viewpoints, organizational structures, and future plans on their Web sites. Commercial firms use the Web to publicize their products and services, and many allow customers to place orders and to complete transactions on-line.

For a large—but hardly representative—segment of the American population, electronic mail (or e-mail) has become the preferred method of routine or casual correspondence among individuals.[1] Nielsen Media Research estimated that in June 1998, some 70 million

---

[1]E-mail correspondence remains the most common on-line activity among people who use the Internet. A recent survey by Forrester Research, Inc., found that among households that had used the Internet at least three times in the prior three months, 88 percent had sent e-mail. No other Internet-related activity was as common. See Bruce Orwall and Lisa Bransten, "Caught in the Web," *The Wall Street Journal*, March 22, 1999, p. R4.

WHAT IS E-MAIL?

Different people mean different things when they speak of electronic mail, or e-mail. In this report, we have adopted an intentionally inclusive notion of what constitutes e-mail. Following the usage of an earlier RAND report (Anderson et al., 1989), an e-mail system is one that

1. Permits the asynchronous electronic interchange of information between persons, groups of persons, and functional units of an organization; and

2. Provides mechanisms supporting the creation, distribution, consumption, processing, and storage of this information.

The ability to address communications to specific individuals or groups is central to our concept of e-mail. Consequently, we do not consider simple postings of information on a Web site accessible to all to constitute e-mail. We recognize, however, that such postings can be precursors of or complements to e-mail communication.

We see e-mail as including not only free-form electronic "correspondence" among individuals and groups, but also more-elaborate arrangements utilizing the capabilities of the Word Wide Web to, for example, post forms to be filled in by individuals and then forwarded to their ultimate destinations. By our definition, multipart documents containing embedded text, video or audio clips, bitmapped pictures, and the like are e-mail.

E-mail is distinct from traditional voice telephony, because the content of voice messages cannot be easily processed or manipulated. Voice recognition software may someday make this sort of processing common, of course, but today it is rare.

In common usage, *e-mail* usually refers to messages sent through the Internet. But direct file transfers from one computer to another can display the two characteristics noted above and, in some applications, can be as effective as Internet-mediated e-mail. Even some transfers of data accomplished by using the keypad of a touch-tone telephone could qualify as e-mail by our broad definition.

Americans, 35 percent of all Americans over 16, used the Internet for one purpose or another.[2]

E-mail is not yet the preferred medium for formal or official communication, however. Although it has become routine to buy books or to trade equities via the Internet, the credit-card bill for those books and the confirmation of that stock trade still come mostly by postal mail. Monthly utility bills and bank statements travel by postal mail. Legal notices, contracts, and other documents requiring signatures are typically sent in hardcopy or by fax.

E-mail is also changing the ways in which citizens and governments interact. In the United States and other industrialized countries, agencies at all levels of government have shown considerable energy and creativity in establishing Web sites. Some of these sites are among the most sophisticated to be found, incorporating effective graphics and powerful search engines and allowing access to huge amounts of government-collected data. Few would quarrel with the proposition that efforts by government agencies to make use of new communication technologies have improved citizens' access to useful information and generally improved the transparency and effectiveness of government operations.

Many citizens routinely e-mail their elected representative to express views on topics of current interest. Politicians and elected officials increasingly use e-mail and Web sites to explain their positions and policies and even to announce their candidacy for elected office. Internet bulletin boards and chat rooms have become forums for discussion of a wide range of public policy issues. Advocacy groups are increasingly aggressive and effective in using the Internet to disseminate their views, to rally support for their causes, and to turn out their voters.

But e-mail is rarely the medium through which individuals carry out personalized transactions with government agencies. They may express personal opinions regarding public issues in e-mail to their congressmen, but electronic queries or filings regarding their own personal circumstances, needs, or activities are still rare.

---

[2]For more on the Nielsen survey, see http://www.commerce.net/research/gideon.

Government use of the Web and the Internet today is, for the most part, restricted to "bulk mail" or, in a manner of speaking, to "wholesale" applications. Reports, bulletins, forms, and statistics that are suitable for all individuals in roughly the same form are posted on Web sites that can be accessed by any individual. Much less common are electronic communications of a personalized or, to continue the above metaphor, "retail" nature—i.e., communications that come from or are addressed to individual citizens and whose content is specific to those individuals. Examples of such communications might be tax filings; applications for various licenses and permits; correspondence related to health, welfare, and retirement benefits; and all manner of queries and responses relating to government programs. Today, this "retail" communication is typically accomplished through postal mail, by telephone, or, occasionally, through in-person contact.

AN UNFINISHED REVOLUTION

Americans have experienced, in a sense, only half a revolution. The Web and the Net have transformed some kinds of communication but have left others largely unchanged. In particular, by limiting their use of the Web and the Net to "wholesale" applications, government agencies are failing to take advantage of what is perhaps the most important feature of these new communication technologies— the ability to communicate at very low cost and almost instantaneously with specific individuals in a format that facilitates copying, forwarding, transcription, checking for completeness and accuracy, and all manner of other processing.

The question naturally arises: Can or should government agencies seek to make greater use of e-mail in their communications with individual citizens? Also, will greater use of e-mail for official or public purposes contribute to a climate in which e-mail can be used more easily or widely for private communications or commercial transactions?

The current communication revolution is incomplete in another important sense as well: Only a part of the American population today has access to e-mail, the Internet, and the World Wide Web. This access is rapidly becoming easier, but convenient use of the Internet and other sophisticated electronic communication channels typically requires a considerable monetary investment for equipment and a considerable temporal investment in learning. Continuing access also requires the services of and in most cases regular payments to an Internet service provider (ISP). Some observers fear that the Internet has widened the gap between the "information elite"—the economically, educationally, and geographically advantaged, who have easy and routine access to all the benefits that flow from being "wired"—and a still significant class of individuals—primarily the poor, the poorly educated, the elderly, and rural dwellers, who all find themselves increasingly isolated and perhaps at a growing disadvantage in economic and social pursuits that depend on easy access to information.[3]

Few doubt that access to the Internet will continue to expand or that someday this access will be as universal as telephone service is today. Questions remain, however, about how long it may take to achieve this near-universal access and what actions and policies might speed the process. More-aggressive efforts by government agencies to communicate with citizens via e-mail may create market conditions, individual incentives, and a public-policy environment that will accelerate the spread of e-mail access. Once again, we are drawn to the questions of how and to what extent government agencies should seek to use e-mail to communicate with their citizen clients.

WHY E-MAIL?

The most obvious attraction of e-mail for interactions between government agencies and citizens is cost. E-mail communication can eliminate the stationery, printing, and mailing costs associated with paper hardcopy communication. Electronic transmission and receipt of information can also reduce processing and handling costs. Information transmitted electronically, for example, can typically be produced from or entered into databases or information systems without the manual transcription required for many paper documents. Similarly, electronic documents can be copied, abstracted, routed, or filed, quite literally, by pressing a key. Electronic docu-

---

[3]For more on the patterns of Internet access and their potential social consequences, see Anderson et al., 1995. Chapter Six of this report provides an updated discussion of Internet access and use in the United States.

ments can be automatically checked for errors or incomplete information and immediately returned to the originator for correction or clarification. Finally, electronic communications can be searched in ways that paper documents cannot be.

Two examples illustrate the size of potential cost savings made possible with electronic communications:

- Since 1988, the Social Security Administration (SSA) has, upon request, provided to individuals a Personal Earnings and Benefits Estimate Statement (PEBES). As the name suggests, this statement summarizes an individual's annual earnings as reported to SSA and the various benefits to which the individual is or will be entitled. Until recently, an individual requested a PEBES in person at an SSA office (by submitting a request form) or by telephone. The requested estimate was printed and then mailed to the individual's address of record. In 1997, SSA experimented briefly with a system that allowed on-line requests for and delivery of PEBESs. The experiment was terminated after a month because of concerns relating to privacy,[4] but it did provide a striking cost comparison. According to the SSA Inspector General (U.S. House, 1997a), "the Agency's shift from mailed hard copy statements to on-line PEBES reduced costs from over $5 per statement to just a few cents. It also provided customers with PEBES statements instantly." Legislation enacted in 1989 and 1990 requires SSA, by the year 2000, to provide an annual PEBES automatically to all workers in the United States who are age 25 and older. SSA estimates that in Fiscal Year 2000, it will issue more than 120 million PEBESs (U.S. House, 1997b). The cost savings that could be realized by delivering even a fraction of these statements by e-mail would be significant.

- The U.S. Internal Revenue Service (IRS) allows taxpayers to file returns electronically, either directly from a home computer or through selected professional tax preparers.[5] The IRS estimates

---

[4]Individuals can still use an on-line form to request a PEBES, but the statement itself is now printed and delivered by postal mail. For more on this experiment and a broader discussion of security in on-line communications, see Chapter Five.

[5]The IRS e-file option does not exploit the Internet. Electronic filers connect their home computers to an IRS computer through a modem and transmit their returns

that in Fiscal Year 1996, the average cost incurred within an IRS service center for processing a traditional, domestic, paper Form 1040 was $3.17. The average cost of processing an electronically filed Form 1040 was only $1.76 (Internal Revenue Service, 1998, Table B).[6] These estimates probably understate the cost advantage associated with electronically filed returns because they do not reflect the much lower error rate found in electronically filed returns. The IRS estimates that 20 percent of paper returns have errors, compared to only about 1 percent of electronically filed returns.[7] Forms found to contain errors require additional processing, and the higher probability that electronic filing will turn out to be "one-time filing" creates a further cost advantage over traditional paper filing.

Although cost savings and easier handling of correspondence are most visible and most easily measured when they occur *within* government agencies, e-mail may produce cost savings, increased convenience, and improved services for individual citizens as well. E-mail communication can, of course, save citizens the costs of postage and the costs and inconvenience associated with photocopying and storing documents. When necessary, citizens will also be able to transmit electronic documents quickly and easily to their lawyers, accountants, advisors, and advocates for advice and assistance in dealing with government agencies.

Requests for information transmitted to government agencies through predictably structured e-mail or Web-based forms may in some cases be processed automatically, without human interven-

---

directly, without going through an ISP. Filing cannot yet be accomplished completely by electronic means. Electronic filers must also file a short hardcopy form (Form 8453-OL) confirming a few summary figures from the electronically filed return and certifying—by providing a physical signature—that the electronically filed return, which does not contain a signature, is complete and accurate.

[6]If the costs of information systems and taxpayer services related to electronic filing are included in these calculations, the costs of paper and electronically filed returns are similar. But IRS officials point out that the volume of electronically filed returns was still quite low in 1996—less than 10 percent of all standard 1040 forms. They do not expect these systemic costs to rise as rapidly as the volume of electronically filed forms. Thus, the lower processing costs associated with electronically filed returns should dominate cost comparisons as the volume of these returns rises.

[7]See IRS Web site, "Questions and Answers on IRS e-file," http://www.IRS.ustreas.gov/prod/elec_svs/ol-txpyr.html#e-file.

tion. The result can be an effective extension of government agency office hours. Citizens can get the information they want whenever they want it. By reducing the cost of access to government-maintained information, e-mail may also make possible significantly improved or entirely new government services for individual citizens.

E-mail can also facilitate communication between government agencies and an increasingly mobile population. Because e-mail is directed to an electronic rather than a physical address, the intended recipient can "pick up" e-mail communications even if he or she is away—even for an extended period—from a primary or permanent address. This may be particularly advantageous for elderly or retired citizens who spend a large part of the year traveling or in a second home or, less fortunately, may be in and out of hospitals, nursing homes, assisted living arrangements, or retirement communities.

E-mail may also make communication easier for citizens with special needs. Web-based forms, for example, can be made available in multiple languages and automatically translated before they are processed by government clerks—a significant advantage for agencies serving polyglot constituencies. Similarly, standardized responses, notices, and statements from a government agency can be automatically translated into the recipient's preferred language. E-mail also has advantages for some disabled citizens. The visually impaired, for example, can use "speaking computers" to "read" e-mail.

For government agencies that must communicate with a large and diverse public, Internet-based e-mail offers important advantages over specialized computer-to-computer forms of electronic communication. The federal Health Care Financing Administration (HCFA), for example, can (and, in fact, does) require health-care providers to install special software and to connect directly to designated computers if they wish to submit claims for Medicare reimbursement electronically. Requiring individual beneficiaries to go to similar trouble to check on the status of specific claims would almost surely be infeasible—especially if, say, the SSA required different software or procedures to link up with their computers, etc. The Internet provides a common standard by which nearly all computers can communicate, and it would surely be foolish for government agencies to seek other protocols through which to communicate with the public at large. As usage of the Internet grows, it may be only a matter of time before even specialized users, such as Medicare health-care providers, demand to use standard rather than specialized protocols.

WHY *NOT* E-MAIL

There are, of course, disadvantages to e-mail communication between governments and citizens. The most obvious of these are the significant costs in both time and money that citizens must incur to establish and to maintain access to e-mail services. Equipment must be purchased and periodically replaced or upgraded; users must purchase and become proficient in using appropriate software; e-mail accounts have to be established and paid for. Today, these costs constitute a barrier to e-mail access for many citizens. But these costs are falling, and access to the Internet and to e-mail services is increasing rapidly, at least in the United States and other industrialized countries. Various options for public Internet access—public-use terminals in libraries, government offices, or social service institutions—are being experimented with.[8] Several vendors already offer free e-mail services, typically relying on advertising revenue to cover costs. The total costs of e-mail access will probably never fall to zero, and some citizens may always be excluded from access, but all indications suggest that access to and use of e-mail are expanding rapidly.

Perhaps a more serious impediment to widespread use of e-mail for communication between citizens and government agencies will be the difficulty of insuring the security of such communication. Many personalized communications between government agencies and individual citizens—tax returns and notices, notices of payment for health care, statements of retirement benefits, for example—contain sensitive information, the privacy of which must be protected.[9] Be-

---

[8]For some examples, see Anderson et al., 1995.

[9]Some proponents of e-mail point out, quite correctly, that there is considerable room to question the security of traditional postal communication between government agencies and citizens. After all, sensitive government communications in envelopes clearly indicating their origin often sit for hours in unsecured mailboxes from which they could easily be removed by anyone so inclined. Further, the deliverer of these sensitive documents, the U.S. Postal Service (USPS), is shielded from any liability arising from lost or misdelivered mail, and a citizen has no right to compensation from

cause some kinds of communications (tax returns and claims for unemployment benefits are obvious examples) are legally binding,
some way must be found to insure the integrity and authenticity of
communications and to prevent later repudiation by the sender. The
technology necessary to justify confidence in the integrity, authenticity, nonrepudiation, and confidentiality of Internet communications
exists today, and a number of private firms already offer secure
e-mail services to clients who need them and are willing to pay for
them. What is lacking today, however, is an administrative infrastructure sufficiently scalable to support secure e-mail communications, potentially, for any citizen who wishes to use such services to
communicate with government agencies.

Of course, not all communications between government agencies
and individual citizens involve the transmission of sensitive information. Creating a national infrastructure for secure e-mail and establishing public trust in the security of e-mail communication will
be massive and possibly controversial undertakings. No one would
seriously argue that government agencies should postpone all efforts
to make greater use of e-mail until the integrity, authenticity, nonrepudiation, and confidentiality of these communications can be assured. Surely, it will be better to begin with relatively undemanding
applications, using these to gain experience before attempting more-
complex or more-sensitive communications. But there should be no
illusions that the need for secure e-mail can be avoided in the longer
run. Almost without exception, the federal and state government
functions that generate the largest volumes of individualized correspondence require the transmission of very sensitive information:
taxation, health and welfare programs, Unemployment Insurance,
Social Security. We return to the issue of e-mail security in Chapter
Five.

Some of the advantages of e-mail can, in particular circumstances,
turn into disadvantages. The speed of e-mail communication is, for

---

USPS for losses suffered as a result of lost or compromised mail. Defenders of
traditional communication modes retort that tampering with mail is a serious offense
and that USPS employs inspectors "with badges and guns" to protect the integrity of
postal mail. However secure traditional postal mail may actually be, citizens and
government agencies in the United States and most other industrialized countries
seem to have agreed that it is secure enough. Such consensus has not been reached
with regard to e-mail.

example, a great advantage. But it may foster unrealistic expectations among citizens about the timeliness of government responses to queries. Also, e-mail is arguably superior to a telephone interaction when a citizen is seeking information on or clarification of some government policy, decision, or benefit, because e-mail can automatically create an easily searched or retrieved record of precisely what was said. (Recording telephone conversations is a much more cumbersome procedure.) The downside to this, however, is that both questioner and respondent may become much more cautious in what they say, closing off opportunities for helpful, if less formal, interactions.

We are not suggesting that e-mail can or should replace all written, telephonic, or in-person interactions between government agencies or employees and individual citizens. Nor are we suggesting that e-mail should become the sole channel for carrying out even selected kinds of official communication. The option to use paper or telephones will, of course, be maintained. In this report, however, we argue that e-mail can offer opportunities for significant improvement in communication between government agencies and citizens and that the very real obstacles to such communication can for the most part be overcome. Consequently, we argue that agencies at all levels of government should seek ways to add e-mail to the communication options they now employ.

A SPECIAL ROLE FOR GOVERNMENT?

The number of people and organizations making use of the Internet and the World Wide Web and the purposes for which they are using them are growing rapidly. As more and more people think of e-mail as a preferred (perhaps *the* preferred) medium of communication, they will naturally expect to be able to communicate by e-mail with the government agencies that serve them. And faced with a demand for e-mail communication, government agencies will almost certainly begin to provide it. Inevitably, government agencies will have to establish procedures and capabilities for e-mail communication, just as they once had to establish procedures and capabilities for telephone communication. Being prepared for e-mail communication will require government agencies to face and resolve a variety of technical, managerial, and legal issues. How directly can or should citizens access government databases? How is sensitive information to be protected? For what purposes will an e-mail communication or an electronic signature be legally binding? And so on.

But is this all that should be expected of governments with regard to e-mail? Simply to get ready for the inevitable day when their constituents will demand e-mail interaction? Will it be enough for governments to prepare themselves to be prudent followers of communication trends that are being driven by private-sector users and to become efficient late adopters of communication technologies already widely used in the private sector? Or should more be expected of governments? Do government agencies have a role to play in shaping patterns of Internet or e-mail usage or in encouraging the spread of Internet and e-mail access? Can or should government agencies play an active role in completing the still-unfinished revolution in communication?

Arguably, the answer to these last questions is yes. Private-sector institutions can and do serve selected populations, populations that desire and, typically, can pay for specific services. Clearly, many Americans—but by no means yet a majority—desire the kinds of services available through e-mail and the Internet and have the ability to pay for them. Access to and use of the Internet and e-mail are growing in nearly all segments of the U.S. population. Nonetheless, some groups remain distinctly "unwired and underserved." Elsewhere, we argue that significant gains would accrue both to individuals and to society at large if access to modern communication technologies were more universal (Anderson et al., 1995).

Efforts by some government agencies to offer services on-line are unlikely to encourage many of the currently "unwired" to seek or to use Internet access. The strongest incentives for people to go on-line will continue to arise from nongovernmental applications—entertainment; shopping; access to weather reports, sports scores, or stock market quotations; and communication with friends and colleagues.

At the margin, though, government efforts to make better use of e-mail may be helpful in spreading access. Government agencies bear an obligation to deal with a wide cross-section of citizens, not just those whose private circumstances allow them access to or predispose them to use the Internet. Nearly everybody pays taxes and renews his or her driver's license. Indeed, some large government programs serve principally the groups who today are least likely to have access to the Internet. The poor and poorly educated, for example, may come in contact with government agencies through income assistance and job training programs; the elderly through Medicare or Social Security. Activities associated with making government services and information increasingly available on-line may gently encourage the spread of Internet access among these populations. Workshops to inform Medicare beneficiaries about new on-line services, for example, might increase their awareness of other uses for the Internet. Efforts to facilitate access to government services could lead to increased investments in public terminals, e-mail kiosks, or free e-mail services—investments that might not be undertaken simply to allow better access to Internet entertainment. And the potential size of government applications of e-mail may also help to create or establish technical and operational standards (for, say, Internet security) that will benefit non-governmental users. By leading the way, government agencies may help to define practices and procedures with wide applicability.

It would probably be unrealistic to expect a government agency to undertake major investments in equipment, software, new proce-dures, training, and public education associated with increased use of e-mail if e-mail does not offer hopes of either significantly reduced costs for the agency or noticeably improved service for its citizen clients. The principal motivation for making government services and information more available on-line will be and should be to im-prove the efficiency and quality of government services. But actions taken by government agencies to streamline or improve their own operations may yield some modest social benefits in addition to the benefits that accrue to the agency in question and its immediate clients. Thus, there seems to be a plausible case for at least some government agencies being "forward leaning" in their decisionmak-ing about e-mail.

THE PLAN OF THIS REPORT

Chapter Two of this report offers a brief review of how agencies at the federal, state, and local levels are beginning to use e-mail in their communications with citizens. We note that to date there appears to have been rather little use of personalized e-mail correspondence.

In Chapters Three and Four, we turn to case studies of two government agencies that exchange very large volumes of personalized communications with individual citizens. The Health Care Financing Administration (HCFA) is the agency of the U.S. federal government that, among other responsibilities, is charged with administering the Medicare program, which provides health insurance benefits to elderly and disabled Americans. The California Employment Development Department (EDD) administers the unemployment insurance program for the state of California. In each of these case studies, we review the various types of individualized correspondence received or sent by each agency and explore the possibility of using e-mail to facilitate these communications. We describe the potential benefits of e-mail utilization and the obstacles that these agencies and their clients will have to overcome if these benefits are to be realized.

In the remaining chapters of this report, we broaden our perspective to discuss issues raised in the two case studies that we believe are relevant to other potential governmental applications of e-mail. Chapter Five deals with the particularly thorny problem of insuring the security of sensitive communications between citizens and governments. This chapter also discusses a number of other issues raised by the prospect of increased government use of e-mail: the need for and desirability of "tokens"—i.e., "smart cards" or other devices that contain information about individual citizens and are used to access on-line government services; problems of maintaining archives and audit trails of electronic communications; managing the expectations of citizens increasingly used to near-instantaneous response in on-line transactions; and controlling unwanted e-mail and inadvertent or malicious threats to the electronic communication channels used by government agencies.

Governments, of course, have responsibilities to all citizens, and support for government use of e-mail will undoubtedly be weakened if large groups of Americans do not enjoy access to this communication medium. Chapter Six addresses patterns of access to and use of e-mail among the American population.

Chapter Seven offers some concluding observations and recommendations.

Chapter Two

THE MEDIUM AND THE MESSAGES:
NOTEWORTHY FEATURES

In announcing a new program of research on "digital government" in 1998, the National Science Foundation (NSF) argued that advanced information and communication technologies could be deployed in ways that "can be expected to contribute to reinvented and economical government services." Moreover, the announcement argued, "as society relies more and more on network technologies, it is essential that the Federal Government make the most effective use of these improvements" (National Science Foundation, 1998).

Until recently, however, most research on uses of network technologies to restructure business interactions and create cost-effective service improvements has been carried out in private sector organizations. Consequently, when we began this study, we could not rely on an established body of empirical literature on the types of individualized interactions between government agencies and their citizen clients. Instead, to guide our case studies, we developed a provisional typology of individualized messages that might be communicated via digital media, along with a set of characteristics that might be expected to affect the utility of those messages for a range of government-citizen communications. Concurrently, we sought examples of extant Internet-enabled communications to populate the typology and illustrate the targeted features. Finally, we undertook an informal survey of state chief information officers (CIOs) or persons in equivalent positions to elicit emerging practices.[1]

---

[1]Several reasons kept us from attempting to do a scientific survey of the kinds of digital communications offered by government agencies. First, not enough systematic

The results of these efforts helped frame our approach to data collection and interpretation in the two agencies we studied in detail (see Chapters Three and Four). We describe them briefly below.

MESSAGE TYPES

As explained in Chapter One, the focus of our study was individualized communications (rather than, for instance, general posting of government information or public discussion forums). Thus, typologies based on areas of government activity where digital network technologies are being applied (e.g., education, business regulation, social services, law enforcement) were not generally helpful.[2]

However, each application area produced a number of instances of the sorts of interactions in which we were interested. We determined that, for purposes of this research, the conceptual framework of greatest utility would focus not on the content or subject matter of messages but rather on their type, where types are based on what kind of interaction the message accomplishes and how the medium itself affects the conduct of the interaction.[3]   Table 2.1 presents the top-level set of distinctions we employed.

---

empirical studies are available to support the design of a sampling framework, even within a single jurisdictional level (e.g., states). Second, the array of offerings is changing so rapidly that any well-defined sample might be obsolete before it could be studied. On the one hand, new public services are announced almost daily. On the other hand, sometimes with less fanfare, services are withdrawn. The termination of citizen interactions with SSA's PEBES system attracted nationwide attention (see Chapter One). By contrast, the demise of Hawaii FYI and Info/California in the mid-1990s, because of state budget cuts, received much less publicity. (See Cranford, 1995; Kennedy School of Government, 1993; Swope, 1995.)

[2]See, for example, Eisenach, 1997.

[3]This pair of distinctions reflects two concurrent and sometimes conflicting lines of research on computer-supported cooperative work (see also footnotes 4 and 5, below). From their earliest work on the Lens system, Tom Malone and his colleagues at MIT have demonstrated how "semiformal" properties of message bodies, when integrated with rules systems, underlying databases, and message agents, can accomplish a significant part of the information-handling work often done by humans. (See, for instance, Crowston, Malone, and Lin, 1986; Lai and Malone, 1988.) In contrast, Terry Winograd, Fernando Flores, and colleagues at Stanford have emphasized performative over information-processing properties of messages. Their work stresses the different kinds of actions that can be accomplished by the language of messages. (See, for

Table 2.1

Message Types and Examples

	Form Based	Free Form
Simple	Opinion polling	Advice giving
Complex	Applying for a business license	Public commenting

Form-Based vs. Free-Form Messages

Most, if not all, messages exchanged in the course of individualized interactions between government agencies and individual citizens can be classified initially into one of the four cells of Table 2.1. The two columns of the table are distinguished on the basis of the extent to which a message body is formally constrained. *Form based* means that the message body is highly structured, that it relies for its formulation chiefly or exclusively on prestructured response fields (for instance, permitting only responses that are selected from a menu of choices or accepting only a limited range of short answers). In contrast, *free form* means that, outside of the e-mail headers, the communication is open ended and not formally prestructured.

This distinction is significant in assessing the potential benefits associated with converting to e-mail many of the traditionally conducted agency-citizen interactions studied in Chapters Three and Four. Most important, it serves as an indicator of the extent to which e-mail based interactions are susceptible to automated processing or to handling by means of rules and agents with access to a database. Many contemporary efforts to manage documents, coordinate work flows, and otherwise improve primary business processes turn on exploiting form-based features of digital interactions.[4]   However, Chapter Three argues that free-form e-mail messages may also carry

---

instance, Winograd, 1987; Winograd et al., 1988.)   A brief summary of the two perspectives is provided in Anderson et al., 1989.

[4]Contemporary research has brought cognitive (form-based) and performative (action-based) perspectives on the role of e-mail messages closer together. (See, for instance, Medina-Mora et al., 1992; Malone, Lai, and Fry, 1992; and the excellent summary in De Michelis and Grasso, 1994.)   Newer approaches to electronic document management also evidence a shift toward viewing the structural components of documents as semiformal elements that can be made to support more automated routing, storage, and management procedures (Bikson, forthcoming).

with them liabilities not associated with more traditional communication media.

Simple vs. Complex Messages

The two rows of the table are distinguished performatively, or by what the messages accomplish.[5] *Simple* messages attempt only to convey information. *Complex* messages, borrowing from Milward and Snyder (1996), attempt to do something more, such as pay a fine, apply for a business license, or carry out some other official interaction. These complexities impose additional kinds of system costs, data requirements, and security concerns that entail special technical features or raise implementation concerns that do not arise with simple messages. If a citizen seeks by e-mail to find out when a particular real estate transaction was recorded, the request is a simple informational one; but if a citizen wants to record the transaction by e-mail, that, in terms of our typology, is a complex interaction probably requiring special technical features as well as institutional procedures.

The simple-complex distinction merits sharper definition in both technical and legal or institutional terms. (Chapter Five works to establish some of the critical characteristics of an infrastructure capable of supporting complex digital interactions as they are envisioned here.) Nonetheless, even in this preliminary form, we found the distinction useful for categorizing the electronic interactions between agencies and citizens surfaced by our survey.[6]

---

[5]The highest-level divisions of the typology we propose, then, fully cross the two distinguishing dimensions of the cognitive and performative conceptions of messaging (see footnotes 3 and 4). That is, columns of the table are differentiated on the basis of the extent to which formal syntactic and semantic properties of the message body facilitate the processing of the information borne by the message; rows of the table are differentiated by the extent to which the message accomplishes actions that go beyond simply conveying information.

[6]Milward and Snyder (1996) propose as a second major categorizing dimension whether the technology links a citizen to information and services of a single organization or to those of a network of organizations. The ability of digital media to provide "one-stop" interaction with a range of different agency functions through a common interface is a critical element in discussions of cost-effectiveness (agencies can gain economies of scale through cooperation on digital service delivery mechanisms), quality improvements (clients need only make one stop to conduct transactions that would otherwise require dealing with multiple geographically separate offices during

Features of Complex Form-Based Messages

While complex messages may be free form (for example, public comments on a proposed land use solicited by e-mail become part of an official process), by far the majority of complex interactions we encountered in our study were form based. For this reason, we sought to identify additional dimensions that might usefully differentiate varied kinds of complex form-based interactions between government agencies and citizen clients. The following are features that appear to be associated with a range of requirements for systems that can support government-citizen interactions.

Financial or other official transactions. Some of the communications we found accomplished transactions that were only financial in nature. Examples include purchasing tickets to a county fair or getting a dog license. In these cases, private information is provided to an agency (name, credit card number, address). However, the interaction does not differ from commercial transactions carried out with private-sector firms, except that in these cases a public agency is the seller.

These types of financial transactions differ from communications that are solely of legal or official import or that combine financial and legal/official transactions. A sizable number of the official interactions surfaced by our search were of the type we think of as "registrations" or "licenses." In some cases, such as registering a motor vehicle, a financial transaction occurs, but so does the conference of other rights and responsibilities. In other cases, such as registering to be on the list of qualified bidders for government construction work, no financial transaction is involved, but the interaction conveys an official standing associated with specific privileges based on bona fide assurances from the offerer. These interactions, therefore, must have record-bearing status.

---

regular working hours), and primary process redesign (shared use of one-stop technology will require that new collaborative procedures be set up across programs and agencies). For all these reasons, the constructs on which one-stop services are based figure importantly in discussions of the use of e-mail communication to provide agency information and services to clients. However, because it turns on so many considerations that go well beyond the nature of the message itself, we chose not to use joint- vs. single-agency production or access as a categorizing dimension for agency-citizen interactions in this research.

Directionality, history, and interactivity. Communications between citizens and government agencies are likely to differ in some respects depending on their direction (citizen initiated vs. agency initiated), interactivity (real-time or other), and history (the extent to which the system supporting the communications relies on previously stored data about the individual involved in the interaction). As our case studies suggest, different issues related to privacy and authentication (for instance) arise depending on whether communications are largely agency initiated (Medicare benefit notices) or client initiated (unemployment insurance claims).

Independent of directionality, as our case studies and other examples show, carrying out a "retail" interaction on-line often entails the ability of the Internet-based program to access a database, find and extract relevant information, and take appropriate action. For instance, the Social Security Administration's (SSA's) provision of Personal Earnings and Benefits Estimate Statement (PEBES) information (see Chapter One) required an on-line query to access a database via a program that would find and extract all and only the earnings and benefits estimates of a particular person and deliver them only to that person. When agency-client interactions require direct access to an accumulated repository of private individual data for their completion, the demands on the supporting system environment become even more stringent. To date, the most common way of authenticating the inquirer has been to request additional personal information (e.g., mother's maiden name) and then cross-match it with information accumulated in a personal history database.

Finally, it should be noted that besides real-time use of a database, communications of the sort discussed here may often rely on interactions with error-checking programs and other applications that help to guide users and assure the consistency of their responses. Such rules-based programs may also be used to generate heuristic responses in real-time to some types of user questions.

Iterations, asynchronous responses, and out-of-band components. The discussion in the paragraphs above generally applies to one-shot e-mail communications or to interactions in which responses are generated in real-time by computer programs that access data and rules. Although a substantial proportion of the communications elicited by our survey are of these types, it is important to note that these do not exhaust the possibilities.

As is clear in Chapter Four, for instance, unemployment insurance claims could constitute the material for an ongoing dialog. Once an initial claim has been filed, the agency-client dialog encompasses six to seven rounds of continued claims, on average. Moving iterative interactions of this sort to e-mail suggests the need for systems that take into account the ongoing status of a conversation not yet complete.[7] That is, besides the general database, there would need to be at least temporary storage space associated with unique, continuing, individual dialogs.

While some interactions may by nature be extended iteratively over time, others may require extension only because they cannot be handled by real-time interaction with a computer program; rather, they may require asynchronous e-mail communication with a human in the loop. Chapters Three and Four both provide examples of cases in which agency clients may undertake communications not formulable in terms that a rule-based system can respond to automatically. In such instances, the network would have to forward the communications to an appropriate agency employee for a response. As with other iterative interactions, the system would need a way to keep a particular conversation "open," and it would have to integrate agency employee responses into the systems that provide responses from computerized agents.

Finally, some official agency-citizen communications may only be completed by out-of-band interactions (i.e., interactions that take place outside of digital media). Even for simple financial transactions, it is often necessary for the on-line interaction to be completed in another medium (e.g., the county fair tickets are picked up at the box office by the purchaser, or the city mails the dog license to the licensee). For more extended interactions involving such services as

---

[7]The developers of The Coordinator were perhaps the first to call theoretical attention to the fact that messages typically are ordered by a higher-level construct, a dialog or "conversation," for instance; and that social or organizational conventions surrounding the action to be accomplished, rather than internal properties of individual messages themselves, typically determine when a series of exchanged messages can be regarded as complete in that system (Winograd, 1987; Winograd et al., 1988; and see also footnotes 3–5, above).

unemployment insurance compensation or welfare benefits, on the other hand, automatic teller machine (ATM)-like components are envisioned.   Unemployment insurance claimants, for instance, might use an agency-provided debit card for withdrawing funds from an ATM account that would be credited at the appropriate time with the amount of payment indicated when the continued claim is filed electronically.[8] Such out-of-band interactions would have to be triggered by official e-mail communications when those communications, by themselves, cannot accomplish the intended agency function.

SURVEY OF OFFICIAL STATE USES OF E-MAIL

For purposes of this project, our survey was restricted to uses of e-mail for carrying out complex interactions between agencies and their clients as defined above. Accordingly, we sent to CIOs in all 50 states an e-mail survey that asked whether the state offered any on-line services to its citizens and whether it posted any on-line forms that could be downloaded, completed, and returned by postal mail. Additionally, the survey inquired about technical, behavioral, institutional, and legal barriers to full use of digital media for official interactions between state agencies and their clients.[9]

Survey Findings

Responses from CIOs or their representatives revealed that only a small number of states have made real progress toward use of digital technologies for full official transactions with citizens. At the time of the survey (summer 1997), many states were using digital technologies to provide public ("wholesale") information on-line. Further, in varied domains such as education, employment, business, taxes, social services, law, and the court system, they were making official forms available on-line that could be downloaded for completion,

---

[8]See the discussion and examples in Milward and Snyder, 1996.

[9]We restricted our survey to states rather than including federal agencies or municipalities because (1) there was no efficient way to sample municipalities in order to surface the small proportion likely to be making noteworthy progress, and (2) we probed federal-level activity in a two-day workshop reported in a separate document (see Neu, Anderson, and Bikson, 1998).

printing, and return by postal mail. But few offered electronic filing as an alternative to downloading and mailing. (Massachusetts stands out as making considerable progress in offering such individualized transactions without requiring out-of-band components such as mailed hardcopy forms.)

Other general findings from the survey can be summarized as follows:

- Virtually all states post forms, including most of their tax forms as well as many business registration forms. Many states allow tax forms to be downloaded for completion but not filed electronically by citizens, but a sizable number of states allow citizens to file their taxes electronically through a third-party trusted intermediary (who charges an extra fee to the citizen for this service). Maryland, for instance, permits such transactions, but it also allows individual citizens themselves to electronically request a time extension for filing their individual income tax returns.

- Many CIOs or their representatives reported that their state Web servers communicate electronically with thousands of people every day. During tax season, the load increases heavily as future filers use the Web site to get forms and instructions. Of all the states, only New Jersey was able to estimate the number of individual interactions with its Web site in 1997. New Jersey then served an average of 106,000 documents each weekday, and about a third of that number on weekends. The state expected its weekday average to total about 180,000 in 1998.

- No states were offering citizens the opportunity to make their applications for social welfare benefits on-line in 1997.

Overall, states differ considerably in the extent to which they have the capability to implement digital technologies in support of a range of government-citizen interactions.[10] And, among those moving

---

[10]The PFF/IBM report cited earlier expresses concern that lagging-edge states may find themselves caught in a downward spiral. If they fall behind in the implementation of technologies that yield fast, effective ways of dealing with bureaucratic processes, they may be unable to attract high-tech or agile businesses. Saddled with increasingly obsolete systems and offering substandard levels of government service

rapidly toward digital government, there is considerable diversity evident in the approaches being taken and applications being implemented.

Electronic Interactions: A Mixed Sampler

For illustrative purposes, we provide a number of examples of electronic transactions between state agencies and their citizen clients surfaced by our survey and broader on-line review. We have chosen them to show scope and variety; they are not regarded as specially significant, unique, or exhaustive.

- California's Department of Fish and Game allows citizens to submit an on-line application to conduct a limited-permit grouse hunt. The applicant's hunting license number must be provided in the application.

- Florida permits citizens to apply for state employment on-line. The applicant's Social Security number is included in the confidential information required by the application. Sarasota County in Florida additionally offers this transaction at the local government level.

- Missouri lets citizens apply on-line for state employment ("Missouri WORKS") plus job-related services (e.g., job search assistance, employment counseling, and job referrals). Registering the application and résumé on-line, moreover, authorizes the state to make the résumé available on-line and grants permission to employers and state service providers to use the résumé to assist applicants in locating job opportunities.

- Kansas has launched a "one-stop" trial that allows business licensing and tax-form filing on-line.

- Oregon encourages individual citizens to order state publications and to file security complaints on-line.

- In Massachusetts, citizens can go on-line to renew their vehicle registrations, pay traffic citations, and order vanity license plates.

---

to an increasingly demanding populace, they stand to lose a lot if they cannot place in the race to become a "digital state" (Eisenach, 1997).

Payment requires a valid driver's license number and a credit card. State income taxes can also be filed and paid on-line using a credit card. In the future, Massachusetts hopes to provide electronic procedures for permit applications, grant applications, submission of bids for public works, and other such transactions.

- In Arizona, citizens needing legal advice can consult Victor, the "cyber-lawyer."[11] Only available via special QuickCourt computer kiosks, the cyber-lawyer application assists citizens with no-fault divorce filings, child support calculations, landlord-tenant disputes, and small claims inquiries. Victor also provides helpful information about bankruptcy, liens, and wage garnishing and enables relevant court-ready documents to be printed. In the future, because of increasing use of the service, Victor will start charging for the production of court-ready documents. Advice will continue to be free.

Barriers to Increased Electronic Communications

As a part of our survey of state CIOs or their counterparts, we inquired about expanding the ways digital technologies can be used to carry out citizen-government interactions. While these technologies continue to advance, even their present-day capabilities are remarkably underexploited by government agency services. Hesitancy on the part of states to move more rapidly into the digital environment can be explained in terms of three classes of barriers.

Security. By far the most frequently expressed concern on the part of state representatives had to do with all aspects of what we call "secure" communication (see the detailed discussion in Chapter Five). Among the security issues raised, privacy appears to be paramount for agency clients. Both government agencies and commercial firms believe that citizens are wary of conducting on-line transactions for fear that third parties will gain access to private information about them (including credit-card numbers, Social Security numbers, and other valuable individual-level data) that could eventually be used for illegal (e.g., fraudulent claims or purchases) or

---

[11]See Perlman, 1994.

annoying (e.g., direct marketing, junk mailing) purposes. Authentication is generally viewed as critical to privacy maintenance and to prevention of the latter sorts of abuses. Finally, legal status issues were raised. That is, electronic transactions not only must meet demands for privacy and authentication but also must be recognized as official and legally binding. Until both parties to the communication have confidence in their security, the ability to accomplish government services to clients electronically will remain severely limited.

Recommendations elicited from state representatives for reducing security barriers tended to turn on legislation and regulation. First, there is a widely perceived need to continue the accreditation of certificate authorities (CAs) (see also Chapter Five). Second and perhaps more important, however, is the need to develop shared accreditation standards that would impose recognized quality controls on public key CAs. While the definition of what constitutes a "suitable guarantee" for an accredited CA is still being debated, a number of states (including California, Washington, Texas, Massachusetts, Pennsylvania, and Utah) are moving aggressively toward the accreditation concept. It is hoped that accreditation will signal quality assurance and facilitate environments conducive to the conduct of government agency business on-line. A third recommendation from many states was to advance the dialog on digital signatures. A digital signature certificate is an encrypted electronic document containing information that verifies the holder's identity, encoded in a highly secure format. Many believe that digital signature certificates will help limit individual citizens' exposure to fraudulent loss in financial or other complex official transactions.

In March 1995, the state of Utah issued the first digital signature act. Under this Utah act, the state assumes the obligation of being a "top level" CA and is charged with policymaking, facilitating the implementation of digital signature technology, and providing regulatory oversight of private-sector CAs through a comprehensive licensing system. Licensing under the Utah act is voluntary; it both confers legal benefits and imposes duties on CAs, subscribers, and relying parties. Specifically, it allocates liability among them while according special legal status to digitally signed documents if the signature is backed by a licensed CA. A number of states (e.g., Washington, Minnesota) have turned to the Utah act as a model for digital signature legislation. Not all legislative bodies, however, are following Utah's lead. California, for example, has rejected the model, enacting a non-technology-specific bill aimed generally at official electronic transactions with government entities. Several other states have also enacted legislation that addresses the authentication of electronic transmissions without presupposing public key methods.

Costs. A second category of concerns relates to cost issues, starting with a shortage of resources to meet current demands. Many state representatives said that faced with increasing demands to make more information and services available on-line, they were already experiencing shortages in such areas as technical personnel, training, hardware, software, and bandwidth—or "everything," as one respondent summarized it. An additional problem is that as state servers quickly get overloaded, catching up becomes more difficult. And an inability to meet citizen needs after an on-line service has been made available creates a host of other costly problems while undermining confidence.

Besides day-to-day costs, a second concern was the ability and capacity of states to manage growth in the demand for electronic information and services. State representatives pointed out that the existing environment will have to be upgraded periodically to deal with increasing numbers of transactions, heightened speed and reliability demands, unavoidable software advances, and eventual requirements for multimedia services. And even the proponents of a public key infrastructure (PKI) for handling security concerns have not assessed the likely costs associated with the maintenance and administration of such a computing-and-communication environment.[12]

Finally, there are substantial technical, organizational, and social start-up costs involved in the introduction of new on-line services. The Massachusetts trial of on-line motor vehicle registration is a case in point. According to the deputy general counsel for the Information Technology Division, at the time of our interviews, electronic registration was costing the state more than it cost to have a citizen come in person to an office for form processing and filing by an employee of the motor vehicles department. Although he could not es-

---

[12]Cf. U.S. Senate, 1997.

timate precisely when it would happen, he indicated that the program was moving toward the point at which Internet/Web-based transactions would be more cost-effective than their in-person counterparts.

Socially constructed barriers. A final category of obstacles to expanded use of digital media for official communication has to do with such socially constructed barriers as technophobia and (dis)trust. According to state CIOs or their representatives, many individuals on both sides of the citizen-government interaction are not necessarily comfortable in computerized environments. Considerable care should be taken to assure that computer-mediated interactions are predictable and intelligible to the humans involved. This responsibility rests partly on the designers of government agency applications and partly on the network service providers who connect individuals to applications. While agencies can improve the functionality of their applications and the interfaces to them over time, the potential influence of network service providers on citizen satisfaction with official electronic communications is less understood and less manageable.

It is also important to point out that the issue of trust is at least as much a social phenomenon as a technical one. Discussions of a secure communication infrastructure sometimes give the impression that trust is either a technical issue to be resolved (for instance, by public key encryption [PKE]) or a legal issue to be resolved (for instance, by new cyberlaws and regulations), or both. But trust is also a matter of public perception. The development of public confidence in interactions with a digital government should be viewed as an evolutionary outcome of accumulated social and technical experience.

DISCUSSION

Because of the rapidly evolving character of network technologies and applications in government agencies today, the typology and review of uses presented here is necessarily incomplete and provisional. From it we therefore draw only quite general conclusions.

First, it is evident at least at the state level that there is considerable variety in preferred approaches to the provision of secure communications. A "one size fits all" solution should not be expected. However, state agencies do share a number of legal, technical, and social/organizational concerns that merit dialog. Establishing venues for exchanging scenarios and procedures, problem formulations, and harmonization of solutions where possible is likely to be worthwhile.

Second, as digital media are being introduced to accomplish complex interactions between citizens and government agencies, laws and regulations will need to change to assure their official status. Currently, it would be premature to suggest any technology-specific legislation. On the other hand, many states could enact legal reforms aimed at paving the way for technological advance. For instance, the Massachusetts General Laws provide 4,515 separate references to documents that must be "in writing," "on paper" and/or signed "in ink." Such phrases, along with references to "original documents," are strewn through the laws and regulations of all states, as well as through those of the federal government and local governments.[13] Their revision could be undertaken in a coordinated and consistent fashion on a jurisdictional basis to remove impediments to digital government transactions as they emerge.

Third, a great many of the practical problems involved in transitioning to digital media as vehicles for official interactions have counterparts now in the research world. For example, a considerable body of research is being directed toward defining and managing digital documents and their components and toward assuring their longevity and usability as material of record (Bikson, forthcoming; Rothenberg, 1995; Bikson and Frinking, 1993). Bringing the two communities into closer proximity could, in fact, be one of the first benefits from the new NSF digital government research.[14] Meanwhile, government agencies at all levels should take advantage of

---

[13]Problems of defining an "original document" in relation to material produced in digital media are discussed in Bikson, 1997, and Bikson, forthcoming.

[14]"There is an immediate opportunity for the broad connection of information services providers and research communities, in an arena drawing heavily on the challenging and unique requirements of the federal sector. Research that considers real world operating constraints can provide valuable new problems and insights for the academic research domain, while demonstrating pilot systems with new capabilities for Federal agencies" (National Science Foundation, 1998).

opportunities to collaborate with or learn from relevant ongoing research.

Chapter Three

CASE STUDY: THE HEALTH CARE FINANCING ADMINISTRATION AND THE MEDICARE PROGRAM

Medicare is a program of the U.S. federal government that provides health insurance for people age 65 or over, the medically disabled, and persons with end-stage renal disease. In 1998, some 38 million Americans were enrolled in the Medicare program. Of these, about 33 million, or 87 percent, opted for traditional fee-for-service insurance (Office of Management and Budget, 1998, p. 220). The remaining 5 million were enrolled in Medicare-qualified managed health-care plans. In Fiscal Year 1998, the cost of the Medicare program was $198 billion.

The overall Medicare program provides two kinds of benefits: Medicare Hospital Insurance (Part A) covers inpatient hospital services, care in skilled nursing facilities, home health services, and hospice care. Medicare Supplemental Medical Insurance (Part B) covers physician services, outpatient hospital services, medical equipment and supplies, and other health services.

The Medicare program is administered by the Health Care Financing Administration (HCFA).[1] Although HCFA sets overall policy for the Medicare program, the actual operation of the program is today highly decentralized. Private firms, usually insurance companies operating under contract to HCFA, perform the day-to-day tasks of claims processing, utilization review, and customer service. Firms

---

[1]HCFA also administers the Medicaid program, a joint federal/state program providing health insurance for the poor. In this report, we focus on HCFA's responsibility for Medicare.

31

that process claims for hospital and nursing home care are called *fiscal intermediaries.* Those that process claims for physician services and other outpatient care are called *carriers.* Generally, there is a fiscal intermediary and a carrier for each state, although some large states have two carriers. Additional specialized contractors process claims for home health care and durable medical equipment in multiple-state regions.

The fragmented nature of current Medicare claims processing can make it difficult to obtain fully up-to-date information about benefits provided or available to specific beneficiaries. Fiscal intermediaries and carriers, of course, maintain records of claims filed with them, but information relating to these claims finds its way into consolidated, programwide databases only with a lag.

In the mid-1990s, HCFA undertook an effort to streamline processing of Medicare claims and to improve Medicare-related information handling. A new Medicare Transaction System (MTS) was to serve as the vehicle for consolidating all claims processing in two regional centers, with a third center serving as a backup. When fully operational, MTS was to support near real-time updating of programwide databases.[2] But as has happened with other ambitious, large-scale information technology initiatives in both the public and the private sectors, MTS development fell behind schedule and costs escalated. In 1998, the project was abandoned. For the foreseeable future, Medicare claims processing will continue on a decentralized basis.

As might be imagined, an insurance program the size of Medicare generates an enormous volume of individualized communications. Both before and after the MTS initiative, HCFA has worked to take advantage of modern technologies in its communications with health-care providers and beneficiaries.

COMMUNICATIONS WITH HEALTH-CARE PROVIDERS

Claims for Medicare benefits are submitted by health-care providers—hospitals, nursing homes, home health agencies, physicians,

---

[2]The promise of MTS and the opportunities it might have afforded for developing new information services for Medicare beneficiaries was a key motivation for undertaking a case study of communications related to Medicare.

etc.—rather than by individual Medicare beneficiaries. For the 33 million beneficiaries with traditional fee-for-service coverage, some 846 million claims were filed during 1997.[3] (Today, claims are not filed for individual services provided to beneficiaries in managed care plans. Reporting of such services was to have been incorporated into the later stages of the MTS development effort.)

HCFA has moved aggressively to convert its communications with health-care providers to electronic formats. The vast majority of Medicare claims today are filed electronically through the Medicare Electronic Data Interchange (EDI). In 1997, 96 percent of all Part A claims and 80 percent of all Part B claims were filed electronically.[4] After claims have been processed, payment to providers is typically made by electronic funds transfers.

COMMUNICATIONS WITH MEDICARE BENEFICIARIES

Since most Medicare-related communications with health-care providers are already accomplished electronically, opportunities for greater use of the electronic media in the management of the Medicare program arise principally in relation to Medicare communications with individual beneficiaries. To date, very few such communications are conducted electronically.

In 1996, HCFA undertook a broad-ranging initiative, called HCFA On-Line, to improve communications with Medicare beneficiaries. Surveys of Medicare contractors identified "top issues" of concern to beneficiaries—i.e., the questions most often asked. A series of focus-group meetings were convened with Medicare beneficiaries in various cities around the country to assess the level of understanding of Medicare benefits and procedures and to identify commonly used sources of information about Medicare. Participants in these focus groups also spoke of the types of information and assistance they needed and the channels through which they preferred to receive

---

[3]See http://www.hcfa.gov/medicare/edi/emcint97 and http://www.hcfa.gov/medicare/edi/emccar97.

[4]See http://www.hcfa.gov/medicare/edi/emcint97 and http://www.hcfa.gov/medicare/edi/emccar97.

information. The focus-group sessions included specific discussion of getting Medicare-related information through the Internet.

As part of the HCFA On-Line initiative, HCFA regional offices and Medicare contractors (fiscal intermediaries and carriers) instituted improved 800-number telephone customer-inquiry systems. Some additional innovative communication arrangements were also tested on a small scale. For example, Your Medicare Center, a small store-front office, was opened in a Philadelphia shopping mall. There, HCFA personnel have direct computer access to Medicare records and can provide real-time answers to questions posed by walk-in visitors. The center also has electronic links to other agencies that serve the Medicare population—the SSA, for example, and the Pennsylvania state Medicaid office.

The most visible result of the HCFA On-Line initiative has been creation of a well-designed and easy-to-use Medicare Web site (www.medicare.gov), which provides basic information about eligibility, enrollment, covered services, preventive health programs, and recognizing and reporting fraud or abuse. A number of key Medicare-related publications are available for reading on-line or for downloading through this Web site, and others may be ordered. The site also provides information about who to contact in each state or territory for further information, customer service, and help related to a specific claim. Through a capability called Medicare Compare, the site also provides information (in a standardized format) on all managed health-care plans available to Medicare beneficiaries in a particular geographical area. The main HCFA Web site (www.hcfa.gov) provides some of the same information for beneficiaries, as well as information relevant to Medicare providers.

Medicare-related information directly available on-line to beneficiaries is of a general nature. Other than allowing a beneficiary to access information about services or administrative offices in his or her particular region, the information is not tailored to particular circumstances. No information is routinely available on-line relating to, for example, a particular beneficiary's benefits or the status of a particular claim. Today, all personalized communication with Medicare beneficiaries is accomplished by postal mail, telephone, or (much more rarely) in-person interactions.

Today, individualized communications with Medicare beneficiaries are of three basic types:

- Initial enrollment in the Medicare program,
- Ad hoc customer service, and
- Notices of claims processed.

We discuss each of these next.

Initial Enrollment in the Medicare Program

Some 3 million new beneficiaries are enrolled in Medicare each year. In most cases (a little under 2 million per year), HCFA uses Social Security information to identify persons nearing their 65th birthdays and sends these persons Medicare enrollment packages. Enrollment packages are also sent each year to about half a million individuals identified by various means as disabled and consequently eligible for Medicare. Each year, another half million or so "walk-ins," individuals whom HCFA has not previously identified as eligible for Medicare, request and receive enrollment packages.

Along with information about the Medicare program, the enrollment package contains a physical Medicare card that identifies the bearer as a Medicare beneficiary.[5] All citizens eligible for Medicare are automatically enrolled in Medicare Part A, which covers inpatient care in hospitals and skilled nursing facilities and outpatient care provided by home health agencies. Beneficiaries pay no premium for Part A benefits. Beneficiaries may also choose to enroll in Medicare Part B, which covers most other outpatient medical services. Enrollment in Part B requires payments of monthly premiums. Because premiums for Part B coverage are quite low, the vast majority of Medicare beneficiaries choose to enroll in Part B. So many choose to accept Part B coverage, in fact, that HCFA has designed the initial enrollment package on the assumption that beneficiaries will do so.

---

[5]The Medicare card is only for convenience. A Medicare beneficiary does not have to produce a Medicare card in order to receive health care. Indeed, there is strong institutional resistance within HCFA to policies that will require any sort of identity card or "token" as a prerequisite to receiving health care. HCFA seeks to instill an attitude of "when in doubt, provide care" among health-care providers.

Beneficiaries who elect to accept Part B coverage need to do nothing. They simply keep the new Medicare cards and begin using them after turning 65. Beneficiaries who choose not to enroll in Part B send the cards back to HCFA with an appropriate form. HCFA sends new cards identifying them as enrolled in Part A but not Part B. Most new Medicare beneficiaries simply do not respond to HCFA.

Customer Service

The contractors that process Medicare claims also have responsibilities for providing customer service: They must answer questions, clarify Medicare policies and procedures, and generally provide assistance and information to Medicare beneficiaries and providers. Each year, Medicare carriers and fiscal intermediaries handle about 15 million inquiries from beneficiaries.[6] In Fiscal Year 1997, the cost of customer service to beneficiaries was in the neighborhood of $65 million.

In the vast majority of cases, customer service is provided through contractor-operated telephone call centers staffed by trained Medicare customer-service representatives and reached through toll-free telephone lines. A much smaller volume of customer service is provided through written correspondence and in-person interactions. The subjects of customer-service calls range from simple administrative matters (such as replacing a lost Medicare card or recording a change of address) to potentially quite complex matters (such as appeals of Medicare payment decisions or reports of suspected fraud or abuse).

Typically, customer-service call centers operate during normal business hours. Most contractors have telephone automated response units (ARUs)[7] that can handle simple matters without direct human intervention. Some contractors have voice-mail capabilities that allow callers to leave messages outside of business hours. And in

---

[6]They also handle a roughly similar volume of inquiries from health-care providers.

[7]ARUs are the seemingly ubiquitous automated telephone systems that allow callers to request various services or information by pressing the keys on a touch-tone telephone: "For information regarding a Medicare claim, press 1. . . ."

regions of the country with significant non-English-speaking populations, contractors offer customer service in multiple languages.

In 1996, HCFA commissioned a survey of its contractors to determine
what kinds of questions beneficiaries and providers were asking. Not
surprisingly, questions and complaints about billing accounted for
37 percent of beneficiary calls to fiscal intermediaries and carriers.
Questions relating to how Medicare relates to other kinds of health
insurance (so-called "Medigap" coverage or Workers' Compensation,
for example) accounted for another 13 percent. Six percent of calls
dealt with simple administrative matters, and another 5 percent were
accounted for by formal appeals of Medicare decisions (Macfadden
& Associates, Inc., 1996).

Notices of Claims Processed

By far the largest volume of individualized communications with
Medicare beneficiaries is accounted for by notices sent by Medicare
contractors informing beneficiaries that particular claims have been
processed and explaining what part of the total bill will be paid by
Medicare and what remains the responsibility of the beneficiary. In
the past, this notification has taken the form of a Medicare Benefits
Notice (for Part A benefits) or an Explanation of Your Medicare
Benefits (EOMB) (for Part B benefits). Medicare is currently in the
process of introducing a new notice of processed claims, called the
Medicare Summary Notice (MSN).

Medicare Benefits Notices and EOMBs are sent whenever claims are
processed, and the volume of these notices has been very large—
around 500 million in 1996. The Health Insurance Portability and
Accountability Act of 1996 (P.L. 104-191, sometimes known as the
Kennedy-Kassenbaum Act) expanded the range of claims that must
be acknowledged by an EOMB.[8] HCFA officials estimate that if they
made no changes in their notification procedures, complying with
the law would increase the combined number of Medicare Benefits

---

[8]Prior to passage of the Kennedy-Kassenbaum legislation, EOMBs were sent only
when the beneficiary was required to pay a portion of the bill. The 1996 legislation
requires that EOMBs be sent for all claims.

Notices and EOMBs to somewhere in the neighborhood of 750 million per year.

Fortunately, by introducing the MSN, HCFA will be able to reduce dramatically the number of notices sent. The MSN is a *monthly* statement summarizing all Medicare claims processed by fiscal intermediaries or carriers during a given month. Nonetheless, when the transition from Medicare Benefits Notices and EOMBs to MSNs is complete, about 300 million MSNs will still be sent each year.[9]

OPPORTUNITIES TO USE E-MAIL

What opportunities are there to make use of e-mail for each of the categories of individualized communications associated with the Medicare program? What benefits might accrue to Medicare beneficiaries and to HCFA if e-mail could be used to supplement current communication methods?

It seems useful to think about these questions in two different ways. The most immediately relevant approach is to ask what role e-mail might play in the operation of the Medicare program, *as it is currently structured.* What kinds of paper or telephone communications, for example, could be replaced, made quicker and cheaper, or otherwise improved by the use of e-mail? Quite appropriately, the first applications of e-mail will be aimed at replicating or replacing other forms of communication, and the early investments in e-mail capabilities will generally have to be justified on the grounds that e-mail allows Medicare beneficiaries and administrators to do the same things in a better way.

In the longer run, though, increased e-mail use may suggest or allow changes in the way that Medicare operates. Thinking about the potential benefits associated with such changes is necessarily speculative. But to ignore the possibility that e-mail could allow or encourage fruitful restructuring or reengineering of current practices would sell the technology's potential short. In the discussions that follow,

---

[9]Successful completion of the MTS would have consolidated Medicare claims processing in two locations and allowed more efficient production of MSNs. Although the MTS initiative has been abandoned, the process of replacing Medicare Benefits Notices and EOMBs with MSNs continues.

we try to note both near-term and longer-term possibilities for using e-mail.

Initial Enrollment in the Medicare Program

As Medicare operates now, there is little opportunity for using e-mail to facilitate initial enrollment. Today, an essential part of HCFA's communication with a new enrollee is the delivery of a physical Medicare card—something that cannot, of course, be accomplished electronically. Most beneficiaries do not have to respond to the communication they receive from HCFA. Those who do respond must send back the physical Medicare card they have received, so e-mail would provide no benefit for them.

As we noted above, however, the Medicare card is principally a convenience. It is not required for a beneficiary to receive care, and as such it is not strictly necessary. One can imagine dispensing with the physical card, providing the information contained on the card to beneficiaries electronically (with appropriate privacy protections), and handling the enrollment process electronically for beneficiaries who have already chosen, for example, to deal electronically with SSA or with other government agencies.

Customer Service

Near-term opportunities to use e-mail as an adjunct to customer-service functions seem to be greater. In the course of this work, we interviewed representatives of ten Medicare carriers about the size and character of their customer-service operations. Carriers to be interviewed were identified by staff in HCFA's central office as being among the more efficient and technologically sophisticated carriers and the ones most likely to have thought seriously about or to have experimented with modern communication technologies. Thus, our sample of ten carriers cannot be viewed as representative of all Medicare carriers and fiscal intermediaries.

The most obvious opportunity to use e-mail in Medicare customer-service operations lies in using e-mail to handle inquiries that today are handled by telephone ARUs. Most Medicare fiscal intermediaries and carriers are at least experimenting with ARUs for handling simpler inquiries.[10]   HCFA encourages this use of ARUs and provides "scripts" for them. Some contractors have written their own scripts, seeking to improve on the HCFA scripts or to provide more services via an ARU.

It is hard to know what fraction of inquiries is successfully handled by an ARU without any human intervention. Most contractors have a good idea of how many inquiries *start* with an ARU. But typically they have no way of knowing whether the caller got the information or the service desired through the ARU.[11] A caller who is not satisfied by the ARU may stay on the line for assistance from a human or may simply hang up in frustration and call back later. But even when a caller stays on the line to speak to a customer-service representative (CSR), the ARU may have performed a useful function—perhaps providing the caller with some basic information necessary to formulate a clear question for the CSR.

Among the carriers we spoke with, experience with ARUs varied considerably. One reported that 47 percent of inquiries were handled by ARUs; three reported that only 5 percent or fewer of beneficiary calls were routed through ARUs. These carriers also differed in the services they offered through ARUs. All that had ARUs allowed beneficiaries to check on the status of particular claims; most also allowed beneficiaries to request a copy of a previously sent EOMB. Other ARU options offered by some carriers included requests for publications, information on deductible amounts, address changes, and various kinds of general information relating to the Medicare program. Some carriers kept their ARUs in operation beyond normal business hours, but a more typical policy was to restrict ARU operation to the same hours that representatives worked so that callers would have the option of transferring to a human if they could not get what they needed through the ARU.

---

[10]Nine of the ten carriers we interviewed maintained ARUs to handle at least some inquiries.

[11]Only one of the carriers we interviewed kept careful track of the number of callers who used the ARU to accomplish something and then hung up without talking to a human.

Most of the carriers we interviewed thought that ARUs could handle between a third and a half of all beneficiary calls.[12] To achieve these levels, however, all agreed that considerable customer education and probably better scripts would be required.

All agreed that Medicare beneficiaries generally do not like ARUs. All the carriers that have ARUs have undertaken programs to inform beneficiaries of the advantages of using the automatic service. But responses to customer-satisfaction surveys consistently show complaints that the ARUs go too quickly, do not offer the right choices, or are too impersonal. The consensus is that beneficiaries prefer to speak to a person. To some degree, this reflects the fact that Medicare contractors typically work hard to train their CSRs to be knowledgeable, patient, and helpful—generally nice people to talk to. More than one carrier suggested that Medicare beneficiaries, who are typically elderly and perhaps socially isolated, sometimes just want someone to talk to.

A Web-based form, filled out by a beneficiary and transmitted to an HCFA contractor, could presumably handle any inquiry or transaction that can be handled by an ARU. Such forms would not offer much cost advantage over calls handled by ARUs, though, since both trigger automated procedures that do not require direct intervention by CSRs.[13]

Web-based forms might allow some improvements in the quality of services available to beneficiaries. Using a Web form, for example, a beneficiary could work at his or her own pace, scrolling back to review or to reconsider an earlier option or looking ahead to see what other choices will be offered. Responses could be adjusted without having to go all the way back to the start of a lengthy audio script. The increased flexibility and easier use of Web forms could allow forms to be more complex than a typical ARU script, offering more options and perhaps handling more-complex interactions than can be performed through an ARU. Web-based forms can also provide links to additional information and thus may obviate the need for

---

[12]One carrier estimated that only 25 percent of inquiries might be handled automatically, but another estimated 60 percent.

[13]A Web form that allows free text inputs and must therefore be interpreted by a human would, of course, be more costly to handle than inquiries routed to ARUs.

callers to speak to a CSR. And if fewer beneficiaries need to talk to a representative, more beneficiaries can be served during hours when representatives are not on duty, effectively expanding office hours. Finally, information returned on-line in response to an inquiry can be printed, saving the beneficiary the trouble of copying down—perhaps incorrectly—information transmitted aurally. The printing of on-line information would also allow more-complete or more-complex responses than could be transmitted by telephone. On line, a beneficiary might access, say, a record of all claims processed in the last year, which would be impossible to do by telephone. And Web forms can, of course, be made available in multiple languages (but since ARU scripts can, too, Web forms offer no particular advantage in this regard).[14]

To the extent that Web-based forms could allow more calls to be handled automatically, some cost savings could result. There is no way today to estimate the size of these savings, but they would likely be small, especially when netted against the cost of the public relations, outreach, and beneficiary education efforts required to explain and encourage use of electronic customer-service options. The real motivation for making more extensive use of e-mail for Medicare customer service functions will be to improve the quality and the convenience of service available to Medicare beneficiaries.

Free-form e-mail inquiries (that is, inquiries that do not have some predictable structure) are likely to provide few benefits. In fact, most of the carriers we interviewed viewed the prospect of receiving increasing volumes of free-form e-mail inquiries with some trepidation. Free-form e-mail communications have to be read and responded to, presumably in writing in a return e-mail, by CSRs. There is no particular reason to believe that representatives would be more efficient responding in writing to written queries than they are in responding orally to phoned-in questions. Indeed, since most of us speak faster than we can type, oral responses are probably more efficient. The carriers we spoke with do a very good job of providing their CSRs with very quick access to almost all information necessary to respond to a caller's questions. Representatives successfully han-

---

[14]Web forms might, in fact, be problematic in foreign-language contexts because of character-set incompatibilities.

dle a very high percentage of calls while the caller is on the line. There is seldom any need for the representative to seek additional information and then to call the beneficiary back. Thus, having a chance to do additional information gathering before responding to an e-mail inquiry would be of little value.

A number of carriers expressed reservations about asking representatives to respond to inquiries in writing. Today, representatives are chosen for their telephone skills, their patience, and their ability to find out what callers (sometimes confused or misinformed) are really trying to ask. Representatives are not chosen for their ability to write clear, concise prose that will stand up to close (perhaps even legal) scrutiny. A written response to a query or complaint leaves a different kind of trail than does an oral explanation over the telephone, and additional training may be required for representatives if written responses become commonplace. Written responses may have to be more carefully hedged and consequently less helpful than their less formal, oral counterparts.

An increased volume of free-form e-mail inquiries could also create difficulties in routing inquiries to the proper office for a response. The decentralized administration of the Medicare program is already a source of some confusion among beneficiaries about where to turn for information. The HCFA central office, for example, cannot answer queries regarding specific claims; the relevant information is available only with carriers and fiscal intermediaries. HCFA has, in fact, not publicized the 800-number for the central office for fear that doing so would result in an increased volume of calls that would just have to be referred somewhere else. One of the advantages of using Web-based forms (at least well-designed forms) for e-mail inquiries is that inquiries could automatically be routed to the correct office. Having once found the relevant form on the Web, the inquirer need never know where the completed form was sent. To send a free-form e-mail inquiry, a beneficiary would have to know the appropriate e-mail address, and some would inevitably get the wrong address. The result would be frustration for the beneficiary and an increased sorting burden for HCFA and its contractors. HCFA staff are understandably apprehensive about opening a new and largely uncontrollable "window" for beneficiary inquiries.

E-mail, either structured or free form, could prove modestly benefi-cial in circumstances where language is a problem. Most carriers who provide ARU scripts have representatives fluent in one or a few languages other than English, depending on the populations they serve. Carriers cannot, of course, offer services in all languages spo-ken within the geographical area they serve, and foreign-language-qualified representatives are not always available when needed. Carriers that serve particularly polyglot populations (in Southern California, for example) supplement their own staff by using special translating services. These translators are available on demand by telephone and are patched into the telephone interaction between the service representative and the beneficiary as needed. As might be expected, this kind of on-demand service is quite expensive. In contrast, an e-mail query in a foreign language might be routed to a translator working "off-line" and not necessarily available instanta-neously. The English version would be passed to a CSR, who would respond in English, and the reply would be sent back through the translator. Most carriers already have text-telephone capabilities for persons with hearing or speech disabilities. Nonetheless, e-mail could offer a useful alternative communication channel for hearing-and speech-impaired beneficiaries.

To summarize, e-mail applications may constitute a worthwhile supplement to currently available customer-service options. The most promising applications are likely to be Web-based forms that allow Medicare beneficiaries to get answers to simple questions (e.g., the status of a particular claim) or to complete routine administrative transactions (filing a change of address, requesting a replacement Medicare card, ordering publications, etc.) without having to speak to a CSR. To the extent that these calls are today handled by tele-phone ARUs, e-mail applications would probably yield little in the way of cost savings. But Web forms or other formatted e-mail may be easier to use than the generally disliked ARUs and may allow fiscal intermediaries and carriers to provide a wider array of automated services. Free-form e-mail queries may be of some value for dealings with some specialized populations (non-English speakers, for ex-ample, or the hearing or speech disabled) but would probably add little to the quality or efficiency of service available to the general Medicare population. Responding to unformatted e-mail—and even getting it to the appropriate office for response—could impose significant new burdens on HCFA and its contractors.

Notices of Claims Processed

The most promising application of e-mail within the Medicare program would appear to be sending MSNs. A recent survey of selected Medicare carriers found that the cost of printing and mailing an EOMB (the rough equivalent then of the new MSN) was about 45 cents. Costs have presumably risen somewhat since 1995. The cost of printing and mailing MSNs should be similar to the costs for EOMBs. In contrast, delivering an MSN by e-mail would cost only a few cents. The very high volume of these notices (about 300 million per year, when they are fully phased in) offers the potential for sizable cost savings if a significant fraction of MSNs could be sent electronically.

MSNs are generated automatically as a part of routine claims processing. Presumably, it would be a relatively simple matter to allow beneficiaries to register with HCFA a preference for either electronic or postal delivery. An indicator of this preference and, if applicable, an e-mail address would be added to each beneficiary's master record. When the claims processing system generates an MSN for a beneficiary who has chosen electronic delivery, that MSN would simply be sent off as an e-mail message. MSNs for beneficiaries who have chosen postal delivery would be routed to a printer for handling in the traditional manner. Of course, no Medicare beneficiary would be forced to receive MSNs by e-mail. Delivery by postal mail would presumably remain the standard, or default, option.

Electronic delivery of MSNs could offer a number of advantages over postal delivery. A beneficiary could, for example, receive an MSN sent by e-mail even when away from his or her home address, a potentially significant advantage for the largely retired Medicare population, many of whom spend extended periods traveling or in a second home. E-mail delivery could also be an advantage in less happy circumstances, when a beneficiary is in a nursing home or other care facility.

A beneficiary may also find an electronic MSN easier to handle. It can, for example, be filed, reproduced, or forwarded to a secondary

insurance payer, an accountant, a family member, or some other assistant or advocate without the beneficiary's having to make a trip to
a photocopier or a mailbox, without—quite literally—the beneficiary's having to rise from his or her chair. This could be a significant
advantage for beneficiaries who find it difficult to move about physi-
cally. If e-mail MSNs are combined with the sort of Web-based customer-service capability discussed above, a beneficiary could easily
request replacements for MSNs lost or inadvertently deleted.

Today's paper MSNs provide addresses and telephone numbers for
correcting inaccurate information or for appealing a Medicare payment decision. An electronic MSN could include a link to a Web
form that would allow a beneficiary to respond immediately and directly if something seems amiss. This Web form could automatically
incorporate relevant information from the MSN, making a response
less burdensome for the beneficiary and presumably reducing the
chance that an inaccurate or incomplete reference will complicate
processing of the inquiry or appeal.

In the longer term, HCFA and its contractors may contemplate going
beyond simple notification that particular claims have been processed, in effect combining elements of the notification and customer-service functions. With some further development of Medicare data systems, it may become possible to offer Medicare beneficiaries on-line access to their complete Medicare histories—a full
listing of claims submitted, processed, and pending. Specific account items might be linked to explanations of relevant Medicare
rules or procedures and to forms for submitting common queries.

IMPLEMENTATION OPPORTUNITIES AND CHALLENGES

Termination of the MTS development effort makes utilizing e-mail
for communication with Medicare beneficiaries more problematic—
technically, bureaucratically, and politically. MTS would have provided a few data hubs to support e-mail transmission of MSNs and
perhaps e-mail-based customer service. In the transition to MTS,
existing contracts with Medicare carriers and fiscal intermediaries
would also have been replaced by new agreements with the opera-
tors of the three MTS sites. This renegotiation of Medicare contracts

would have created a natural opportunity to redefine the services offered by Medicare claims processors and the channels through which information is delivered to beneficiaries.

Without MTS, efforts to make greater use of e-mail for communicating with Medicare beneficiaries will have to proceed piecemeal. Contractual arrangements that would allow, encourage, or require carriers and intermediaries to offer e-mail-based services would have to be negotiated with each of Medicare's more than 70 contractors. Because carriers and intermediaries do not all use the same kinds of data systems, multiple software and hardware packages would likely have to be developed to support e-mail communication. And the inevitable start-up and training costs associated with introducing new communication options would be incurred repeatedly in multiple small-scale installations rather than in three centralized operations. Clearly, the continuation of decentralized claims processing and customer service will not improve the efficiency of efforts to introduce greater use of e-mail.

Even more problematic may be the possibility that Medicare-related services may not be uniform for all citizens. All carriers and fiscal intermediaries may not be willing or able to offer e-mail communications to beneficiaries. Even though the Medicare program is administered locally, it is intended as a national program providing similar benefits for all eligible U.S. citizens. To offer additional service options for some citizens—even if these are just communication services—without a plausible prospect that such services will become universal within a few years will be politically problematic, if not impossible.

It may nonetheless be possible for HCFA to embark on a region-by-region program with the eventual aim of providing e-mail communication options for all beneficiaries. Indeed, in the early stages of such a program, the decentralized administration of Medicare may even prove a benefit, creating useful opportunities for smaller-scale testing of various e-mail communication techniques along the way to developing a truly national system. A few of the more technically sophisticated carriers might, for example, be commissioned to test different approaches to the use of e-mail and to the beneficiary education that will undoubtedly have to accompany any widespread use of e-mail. These early tests may help to create standards for service that can be incorporated into future contracts for Medicare claims processing and customer service.[15]

But before even limited tests of e-mail communications can be undertaken, a number of key obstacles must be overcome.

Beneficiary Acceptance

Perhaps the most obvious question to ask is whether Medicare beneficiaries want or would make use of e-mail communication relating to Medicare. No one seriously proposes, of course, that beneficiaries would be required to use e-mail to communicate with HCFA or with HCFA contractors. Postal and telephone communication would remain available, and, indeed, HCFA has plans to improve 800-number telephone access. The question is whether enough Medicare beneficiaries would be interested in e-mail communication to justify the effort and the expense of creating this option.

For current Medicare beneficiaries, the answer is almost certainly no. In 1997, HCFA commissioned focus-group discussions with Medicare beneficiaries to explore a variety of questions generally related to how beneficiaries get and would like to get information about Medicare (Forsyth and Edwards, 1997). Attitudes toward computers and the Internet were specifically explored. Not surprisingly, few current beneficiaries have much experience with computers or the Internet. This is consistent with Census Bureau findings that access to and use of computers and Internet services are much less common among the elderly in America than among other age groups. (See Chapter Six.) Most participants in the HCFA-sponsored focus groups appeared open to the idea of getting information through a computer, but many raised concerns about threats to privacy and about the costs (both to the beneficiary and to the Medicare program) of computer-mediated communication. Even if these concerns were addressed, however, it seems unlikely that a population that rarely uses computers and the Internet for any purpose (at least in comparison to the rest of the population) would derive much

---

[15]Through its Digital Government program, the NSF is now seeking to encourage research and experimentation on information services for citizens (National Science Foundation, 1998).

benefit from being able to access Medicare-related information through these media.

But of course the population of Medicare beneficiaries is not static. As the current generation of American workers ages into Medicare eligibility, there will be a growing population of beneficiaries who became accustomed to computer use during their working careers. It would be surprising if the enthusiasm for e-mail and the Internet that is evident among this population were to disappear when these workers retire. Although it is hard to know precisely when, HCFA will eventually find itself dealing with a population of Medicare beneficiaries accustomed to transacting many kinds of business on-line. These beneficiaries will likely appreciate and perhaps demand a similar ability to deal with Medicare, their principal health-insurance program, on the same basis.

If for no reason other than to prepare for that day, it would probably be wise for HCFA to begin exploring options for e-mail communication. A case might also be made, though, for more aggressive action by HCFA. To the extent that government use of e-mail may serve as an incentive for individual citizens to become "wired," government services targeted on the elderly and the disabled (precisely the Medicare population) may offer particularly attractive applications. Because the elderly and the disabled sometimes suffer a degree of isolation from the rest of society, the potential benefits of being "wired" may be particularly great for these groups. For someone leaving the work force, and possibly his or her previous point of connection to the Internet and e-mail, access to some key government services on-line might be a significant consideration in deciding whether to establish or to maintain independent access to e-mail. On-line availability of Medicare-related information alone is unlikely to tip the balance in many cases, but a general pattern of government services on-line might make a difference.

The Problem of Security

The most difficult challenge along the path to increased use of e-mail for Medicare-related communication will lie in safeguarding the privacy of sensitive medical information. An MSN, for example, contains detailed listings of physicians visited, procedures performed, and tests administered (although, of course, not the results of the tests). In many cases, an MSN can provide an adequate basis for drawing conclusions about a beneficiary's health—conclusions that many beneficiaries would prefer to remain private. Similar information can be transmitted during customer-service interactions. Quite correctly, HCFA attaches a very high priority to protecting sensitive information and will not create new channels of communication not widely accepted as secure.

Today, HCFA and its contractors protect sensitive information principally by mailing such information only to a beneficiary's address of record. Although procedures vary somewhat from contractor to contractor, telephone callers who request potentially sensitive information are typically required to provide some verification of identity—usually a name, SSN, and date of birth, and sometimes the date of a particular service. Medicare beneficiaries who are unable to conduct transactions on their own behalves can authorize some other person to receive information relating to their care, but Medicare contractors typically require prior registration of such beneficiary advocates.

At a superficial level, similar procedures could be applied to e-mail transactions. Communications could be sent only to an e-mail address of record, and individuals requesting information could be required to provide the same information that telephone callers provide. Few view such protections as adequate, however. Indeed, current HCFA policy explicitly prohibits communication of sensitive information by Internet-based e-mail.[16]

Postal mail can, of course, be stolen from a mailbox, and telephones can be tapped. But doing either without the necessary authorization is a serious crime, and perpetrators are subject to severe penalties if caught and prosecuted. Today, e-mail communications enjoy no

---

[16]As noted above, HCFA does allow health-care providers to file claims for Medicare reimbursement via the Medicare Electronic Data Interchange using a direct computer-to-computer connection that does not make use of the Internet, thereby reducing opportunities for unauthorized interception. Also, because this computer-to-computer communication is one-way, problems associated with establishing the identity of the electronic correspondents are minimized. The health-care provider sends sensitive information to the HCFA contractor by dialing an established telephone number. The contractor does not send any sensitive information back and thus does not need to establish the identity of the provider.

such legal protection.[17] Perhaps more worrying is the possibility that e-mail communications can—in theory, at least—be easily scanned for the specific bits of information that an eavesdropper may be seeking. A malefactor who has succeeded, for example, in gaining access to someone else's electronic mailbox could capture the next communication with HCFA with a degree of ease and automaticity impossible with postal mail or telephone traffic.

In this legal and technical environment, the security of even one-way communications initiated by HCFA—sending MSNs by e-mail, for example—is problematic. Some combination of legal and technological measures will be required to increase confidence that a message sent by HCFA will be read by only the intended recipient.

Insuring privacy will be even more difficult if electronic communication becomes two-way, with beneficiaries requesting information and receiving sensitive information without a human in the loop. For these applications, some means will have to be found to verify the identity and *bona fides* of the inquirer. Simply asking for personal information such as name, date of birth, and SSN will almost certainly be inadequate. Disaffected children, siblings, or former spouses often know this kind of information and may choose to use it for mischievous or malevolent purposes.

Arguably, sensitive information that is accessible on-line, perhaps without a human in the loop, will require more-stringent protection than similar data that can be accessed only by a telephone or written request. It is, of course, possible today for someone knowing a modest amount of personal information about a few individuals to mount small-scale invasions of privacy, gaining unauthorized access to sensitive information regarding those individuals. Although a specific individual whose privacy is violated may suffer considerable harm, the scale of such violations is limited by the laborious process of requesting information.

The new danger inherent in electronic access to medical information is that very large-scale violations may become possible. The kinds of information commonly used by HCFA contractors to establish

---

[17]Indeed, most e-mail communications are discoverable in legal proceedings because they are presumed to be public.

identity today (names, addresses, SSNs, dates of birth, etc.) are contained in many electronic databases, most of which have no connection to Medicare and over which HCFA exercises no control. (Consider, for example, employment records, credit histories, insurance records, driver's license lists.) If this information were all that was needed for electronic access to sensitive Medicare information, an unscrupulous and technically competent operator with access—authorized or otherwise—to other databases could conceivably access and download sensitive information about thousands or millions of Medicare beneficiaries almost instantly.[18]   Considerable damage could be done in a matter of minutes, probably in much less time than the guardians of the sensitive data would need to recognize what is going on and take steps to stop the outflow. This possibility suggests that beneficiary-initiated requests for sensitive information need to wait until some more secure method for establishing the identity of the requester is available.[19]

A combination of the above concerns was sufficient to force SSA in April 1997 to abandon an experiment in making Personal Earnings and Benefits Estimate Statements (PEBESs) available on-line. On-line requesters of PEBES had to provide exactly the same information required of someone who makes an in-person request at an SSA office: name, date of birth, SSN, and mother's maiden name. Nonetheless, public outcry over the perceived threat to privacy was such that the experiment was abandoned after only a month.

A system of secure e-mail, with at least the potential to be expanded to serve any citizen who wishes to use it, will be a prerequisite for any use of e-mail for transmitting sensitive Medicare-related information. This system will have to allow encrypted transmission and, if two-way communications are to be permitted, will probably have to provide for some means of identity authentication that does not depend on such easily obtained information as SSN and date of birth.

---

[18]Detailed information about the health of large numbers of beneficiaries could be of considerable commercial value, particularly if the mere possession of such information is not illegal. A less than entirely scrupulous pharmaceutical company might, for example, pay handsomely for a list of patients with particular conditions, the better to target a direct-mail advertising campaign.

[19]One approach to authenticating a request for information, a so-called public key infrastructure (PKI), is discussed in Chapter Five.

And a major public relations effort will certainly be required to convince the public that e-mail communications can be made sufficiently secure for transmitting health-related information. Legal changes to extend to e-mail at least some of the protections that apply to postal mail and to telephone communications may also be necessary.

Also helpful (and probably necessary) will be a mechanism that allows individual beneficiaries to choose whether sensitive information regarding their health care is to be transmitted electronically or made available on-line. The idea would be for beneficiaries to be able to declare that their personal information should not be transmitted electronically to anybody, no matter what verification procedures or safeguards have been put in place. Presumably, the burden will be on citizens who wish to enjoy the benefits of electronic transmission to "opt in" to a system that allows electronic transmission, as opposed to forcing citizens who wish to rely on traditional communication channels to "opt out" of the electronic system. To do otherwise would make a system of electronic communication that some citizens may find highly convenient vulnerable to complaints from other citizens that sensitive information was put at risk without the informed consent of all citizens affected.[20]

We argue in Chapter Five that there are no significant technical obstacles to building a system for secure e-mail that meets all of the above requirements. What is lacking is the administrative and institutional infrastructure to manage and support such a system. In current HCFA thinking, a system secure enough for communicating sensitive health-related information will require personalized electronic keys.[21] Creating a system to assign and administer such keys

---

[20]SSA's on-line PEBES experiment was criticized precisely because it required individuals who did not wish their Social Security records to be accessible on-line to opt out of the on-line reporting arrangement, rather than requiring those who wished such access to opt in.

[21]The Kennedy-Kassenbaum legislation of 1996 (P.L. 104-191) explicitly requires that the Secretary of Health and Human Services "in coordination with the Secretary of Commerce, shall adopt standards for the electronic transmission and authentication of signatures" with respect to transmission of a variety of sensitive health-related information, including health care payment and remittance advice and health claims status. HCFA Internet use policy currently requires authentication of both ends of communications involving individually identifiable health information.

on a massive scale will be a major challenge, clearly beyond anything that could or should be developed by HCFA alone. A secure e-mail system suitable for sensitive communications between citizens and a variety of government agencies will have to grow out of a larger effort involving multiple government agencies and private entities with an interest in secure e-mail communication.

Other Challenges

Efforts to make greater use of e-mail for communication between Medicare contractors and individual citizens will face additional operational challenges. Three in particular stand out.

The constancy of e-mail addresses. Maintaining an accurate and up-to-date file of addresses of record is a key element of many efforts to protect the privacy of sensitive data. Today, for example, Medicare-related information is mailed only to a beneficiary's address of record. Fortunately, citizens typically do not undertake changes in postal addresses lightly. Usually, some significant inconvenience (the moving of household goods, etc.) is associated with a change of postal address, and the frequency of such changes is naturally limited.

The same may not be true of e-mail addresses. Changing ISPs (and associated e-mail addresses) can be accomplished with a single telephone call. The market for Internet access is still in considerable flux; new providers of access and new technologies to support access (e.g., wireless access, access through a cable modem) appear frequently; and prices for Internet access are frequently adjusted. In these circumstances, it would not be surprising if Internet users changed their e-mail addresses frequently. (We know of no reliable statistics on the frequency of these changes, but everyday experience suggests that such changes are frequent. The reader need only consider the number of his or her friends or business associates whose e-mail addresses have changed in the last year.)[22]

----

[22]For an interesting discussion of "churning" among Internet users, see Katz and Aspden, 1997a.

The problem of changing e-mail addresses may be particularly difficult for the Medicare program. Many citizens become eligible for the Medicare program just as they are retiring from the work force and leaving jobs that had previously provided them with e-mail service. E-mail addresses may be particularly fluid for this population. Increased use of e-mail would require HCFA and its contractors to maintain up-to-date files of e-mail as well as postal addresses, potentially a significant new administrative burden.

An alternative might be to require that ISPs routinely provide mail-forwarding services for some specified length of time after a change has been made, much as telephone service providers provide call forwarding today. Such an approach, however, would add regulation to an industry that has thrived and become useful at least partly because it is unregulated; why tamper with a formula that has worked well so far? Message forwarding may also be impractical if some time passes between the discontinuation of service by one provider and the establishment of new service by another. How will the former provider know what the forwarding address should be?

A bolder but perhaps more effective approach would be for some agency (some have suggested the U.S. Postal Service [USPS] for this function) to establish a unique and unchanging e-mail address for each citizen. When signing up with an ISP, a customer would inform the provider of his or her government-provided address. This address would serve as an alias for whatever other address is assigned by the service provider. Any e-mail sent to the government-provided address would reach the intended recipient even if he or she changed ISPs. We return to this notion of universal e-mail addresses in Chapter Seven of this report.

Spamming. Citizens occasionally believe that they have been treated unfairly or unsympathetically by HCFA or by the Medicare contractors. In a few cases, aggrieved citizens have sought to take some sort of revenge. Unfortunately, the opportunity for citizen-initiated e-mail communication with HCFA and its contractors could create new opportunities for disgruntled citizens to disrupt Medicare operations. Particularly troublesome could be "spamming," which in this case would amount to sending very high volumes of e-mail traffic, thereby tying up Medicare computers and making e-mail access impossible for citizens who wish to carry on routine communications. Some technical protections against spam are possible, but the only fully effective defense would be for HCFA and its contractors not to accept incoming e-mail at all—hardly an ideal solution if the original aim was to increase communication options. This issue is discussed more fully in Chapter Five.

Misrepresentation. All of us have experienced the minor annoyance of receiving junk postal mail that comes in an official-looking envelope. If HCFA or Medicare contractors communicate via e-mail, it would not be surprising if junk e-mail designed to look at least superficially like official communications were to follow. Although some technical approaches can make such masquerading more difficult, there is probably no way to prevent it completely. Some legal provision should probably be made to preserve distinctions between official and nonofficial e-mail, some electronic equivalent of the "For Official Use Only" notation on envelopes used by government agencies.

A WAY FORWARD

The above considerations suggest that HCFA might do well to begin experimenting with e-mail communications with Medicare beneficiaries. A promising place to start would be to provide MSNs via e-mail for beneficiaries who desire such a service. The volume of MSNs is large, and the cost differential between hardcopy and electronic versions is significant. Because communication would be one-way, HCFA and its contractors could avoid many of the problems associated with establishing the identity of a requester. The failure of efforts to create a new centralized MTS complicates the introduction of e-mail communications, but some progress should still be possible. The current decentralized approach to Medicare claims processing provides a basis for testing e-mail communications on a small scale before attempting to offer such communication options nationally.

Safeguarding the privacy of sensitive data will be a serious but technically soluble challenge. The principal impediments to a national system of secure e-mail are administrative and institutional, and plausible approaches to overcoming these impediments are available. HCFA will have to work with other government agencies to create the administrative infrastructure necessary to support a potentially national system of secure e-mail.

HCFA's communications with its Medicare partners (carriers, fiscal intermediaries, managed health plans, etc.) could provide useful test beds for Internet security arrangements. Large volumes of sensitive data are routinely moved between HCFA and these partners today, although not via the Internet. Many of these partner organizations are technologically sophisticated and possibly well suited to testing early versions of Internet security protocols. Experience gained through tests within this limited circle of actors may help to identify techniques that can eventually be made simple and robust enough for use by the general Medicare population.

Beneficiary-initiated e-mail communications will pose more-difficult problems. At the very least, Web forms will have to be developed to support formatted inquiries and requests for information, which ideally will be processed and responded to automatically. Unformatted inquiries will offer few advantages over telephone inquiries for beneficiaries, HCFA, and HCFA contractors, and they will probably offer some disadvantages. Some modest benefit may lie in being able to use less-expensive, off-line translation services for dealing with beneficiaries who do not speak English. The disadvantages of unformatted e-mail inquiries may more than overshadow these benefits, however. The two most worrisome disadvantages may be unrealistic expectations on the part of beneficiaries and the need to train CSRs to provide written responses.

Beneficiary-initiated communications will also complicate privacy-protection efforts. Unless responses are sent only to an e-mail address of record, ways will have to be devised to verify the identity of inquirers. Probably, some form of digital signature system will be required (see Chapter Five for more details). And beneficiary-initiated communication will create vulnerabilities to spamming that would not have to be faced if HCFA restricted itself to send-only uses of e-mail, such as using e-mail to deliver MSNs.

The highest priority, then, for HCFA may be to cooperate with other government agencies to develop a mechanism for secure and reliable delivery of MSNs by e-mail. Beneficiary-initiated e-mail interactions might best be postponed for a few years while HCFA gains experience (technically, institutionally, politically, and with regard to public acceptance) with less-demanding forms of e-mail communication. A delay of a few years will also allow further progress to be made toward developing an infrastructure for truly secure two-way communication and for verifying the identity of e-mail correspondents.

Chapter Four

CASE STUDY: CALIFORNIA'S EMPLOYMENT DEVELOPMENT DEPARTMENT AND ITS UNEMPLOYMENT INSURANCE PROGRAM

The Employment Development Department (EDD) acts as California's state employment security agency, administering its unemployment insurance (UI), job service, employment tax, and disability insurance programs. A joint federal/state effort, UI was implemented nationwide in the 1930s as a community-based short-term wage replacement program.[1] In California today, over 28 million claims of varying types are filed annually for UI benefits.

Like our first case study, the federal Medicare program (which is decentralized because it is operated by varied carriers or other fiscal intermediaries), UI is also a highly decentralized program. It is based on federal law but executed through state law and by state employees. Thus, its implementation reflects differing state provisions; for example, states have varying rates for employers' UI tax contributions. Implementation is also influenced by different state laws; for instance, California state law includes the right to privacy, which results in stronger privacy protections for individual-level data than exist in many other states.

Across states, however, UI differs programmatically from Medicare in a number of respects that are significant from the point of view of this study. For instance, UI activity in all states largely involves

---

[1] Refer to California Employment Development Department, 1996b and 1994. Other background information is available online at http://www.edd.cahwnet.gov.

clients who interact directly (rather than through intermediary organizations) with the program. They do so on a frequent but time-
limited basis, and, at any given period, a substantial proportion of
the clients are repeat customers. California's UI program thus represents a relevantly different case study context—both jurisdictionally
and in other ways—within which to pursue questions about the potential benefits and obstacles to e-mail communication between
government agencies and their citizen clients.

STUDY PROCEDURES

Information for this case study comes from a number of sources.
First, project team members made several working visits to EDD to
conduct interviews and gather documents. While most of our time
was spent with members of the operations branch concerned with
providing oversight, data, and support for the UI Division, we also
interviewed representatives of other organizational units with relevant functional responsibilities (including the information technology branch, employment and training branch, tax branch, information security office, and legal office).[2]

Besides interview information and documentary material, we sought
quantitative data related to types of claims filed and characteristics
of claimants and claims processing. For this purpose, we focused on
calendar year 1996, the most recent year for which complete data
were available at the time of our interviews.[3] EDD provided us with
the requested data extracts, formatted as an Excel Workbook comprising nine worksheets, and with supplementary data available at
the University of California at Los Angeles (which receives copies of
mandatory Department of Labor reports submitted by EDD). The

---

[2]Gretchen Jung, who headed the Oversight, Data and Support Section of the UI
Division, and Talbott Smith, Chief of the Administrative, Workforce and Enterprise
Solutions Section, Information Systems Division, provided us with most of the data
and documents used in this chapter.

[3]We chose calendar year rather than fiscal year because, of the two types, calendar-
year data were complete and could more readily be compared with data from other
sources. But however the time period is bounded, it will include some UI continued
claims initiated in the preceding period as well as some initial claims whose continued
efforts persist into the next period. So "complete" should not be taken to mean that all
individual claims-related interactions represented in the focal year were completed.

data and reports provided the information base for the quantitative findings reported below.

Additionally, we made a working visit to the Information Technology Support Center (ITSC), which is housed at the University of Maryland and operated jointly by the university, the state of Maryland, Mitretek Systems, and Lockheed Martin. ITSC receives support from the Department of Labor, the state, and other sources to carry out information technology projects that will assist state employment security agencies. There we interviewed individuals conducting ITSC's studies of emerging technical options to support UI claims filing, including prototype and pilot projects that rely on Internet/Web-based procedures.[4] Together with the sources consulted in the overview of state-level electronic interactions summarized in Chapter Two, ITSC interviews and reports provided a broader frame of reference for viewing the California EDD case.

BACKGROUND AND PRESSURES FOR CHANGE

As a short-term wage replacement program, UI was predicated on the assumptions that most individuals would remain with a single employer for long periods of time and that episodes of unemployment would be rare and brief (California Employment Development Department, 1994).[5] These assumptions, however, are no longer valid. For instance, in California it is estimated that on average people will change jobs seven to eight times during their working life and that (given rapid technological advance) these changes may involve occupational change as well. Industry change and skill obsolescence (in combination with other factors) mean that California's population has come to include growing numbers of individuals who are frequently or chronically unemployed.

In response to conditions like these, a 1993 unemployment compensation amendment mandated all states to implement a system for profiling initial UI customers to determine which individuals are most likely to exhaust their benefits and require more intensive

---

[4]For up-to-date descriptions of ITSC projects and related reports, see http://www.itsc.state.md.us.

[5]See also California Employment Development Department, 1996e.

reemployment efforts to help them return to work sooner. Those who meet the "profile"—in California, an estimated 8 percent of all initial claimants—are to be given personalized services tailored to their initial needs and circumstances. More recent welfare-to-work initiatives also create additional clients for EDD who need job services. While intended eventually to reduce the number of individuals dependent on government programs, such legislation has strained EDD's limited resources.

Finally, urban sprawl, population diversity, and other conditions mean that in-person, locally based UI services do not well serve California's present needs (California Employment Development Department, 1994). Together with increased costs of physical facilities and decreased federal funding, the circumstances outlined above have given rise to pressures for change in California's UI delivery system.

These pressures, to be sure, are not unique to the UI program. In varying ways they bear on a considerable number of state-delivered services to citizens. There are, however, new information and communication technologies that appear able to address at least some common dimensions of these problems. Consequently, in 1995 the California Governor's Council on Information Technology issued a set of recommendations to state agencies stressing ameliorative roles for digital media. In particular, the council urged agencies to use information and communication technologies both to improve efficiency and effectiveness of government operations and to improve public access to government information and services (Governor's Council on Information Technology, 1995).

Accordingly, EDD took as a primary goal the provision of greater direct public access to its information and services. This goal was targeted via two objectives that were to be reached through the broader deployment of digital media: to gain efficiency by reducing and/or redirecting staff work efforts, thus coping better with economic change and limited resources, and to increase customer service quality and satisfaction by providing self-service options (resulting, for instance, in faster and more readily available service). Both objectives are equally valued by EDD and are used to inform and evaluate its strategic technology decisions.

In view of the very large volume of individualized claims-related communications the UI program generates, use of electronic media could contribute significantly to the realization of these objectives. Likewise, because it accounts for the largest proportion by far of EDD's total volume of retail interactions, the UI program affords an ample base for exploring the consequences of transferring at least some of these interactions to contemporary networked technologies. We next describe that communication environment in more detail.

COMMUNICATIONS RELATED TO UI CLAIMS

As explained earlier, UI services have historically been delivered on a local in-person basis through one of EDD's 157 California offices and branches. In the first half of the 1990s, when the unemployment rate was higher, initial UI claims totaled over 4 million a year. As unemployment rates decreased later in this decade, the number of initial annual claims decreased as well. In 1996, which serves as the focal year for this case study, just under 3.5 million initial claims were filed.

In periods of relatively low and stable unemployment such as California has experienced in recent years, it is estimated that 60 to 70 percent of initial claimants will be repeat customers—that is, individuals with prior episodes of unemployment for which UI claims were filed and benefits received (e.g., seasonal employees, construction employees, film/TV industry employees). Valid initial claims are followed by subsequent biweekly continuing claims, so long as the claimant remains unemployed and eligible for benefits and continues to look for work. A claim can continue for a maximum of 26 weeks, unless an extended benefit program is in effect. On average, an initial claim generates six to seven continuing biweekly claims, yielding a total of about 23.5 million continued claims per year.

Individualized interactions associated with the traditional UI claims process can be summarized as follows:

1. An initial UI claim form is picked up, completed, and turned in at an EDD field office by the claimant. (The employer will have reported the separated employee, by Social Security number and wage rate, to EDD's tax branch.)

2. An interview with field office staff personnel most often results in a routine monetary decision about eligibility for benefits. Field office staff enter relevant client data (obtained from the form plus the interview) into a centralized UI database.

These first two steps may have to be repeated. In some cases, clients either lack some of the information required by the form or make mistakes in providing it. The most commonly missing or incorrect items on initial UI claim forms are the correct name and address of the former employer and the work dates and wage amounts needed to calculate base period earnings (for purposes of determining eligibility and benefit amounts) (California Employment Development Department, Project Management Division, 1995).[6]

It thus may take several trips to a field office before a claimant has information that is both complete and correct for filing purposes. On average, EDD field staff representatives spend about 33 minutes on each initial application. The time is taken up with aiding clients as they complete the form, asking questions to obtain additional information as required, and entering and processing the resulting data in the UI computer system. These time estimates also include clerical support and supervisory effort in addition to field interviewer time.

3. If an initial claim form appears to be complete and correct but raises questions that field office staff cannot resolve (typically, more-complex questions about eligibility), a telephone interview is scheduled with an adjudication staff member. Nonmonetary determinations must be completed in all such cases, which amount to about 1.2 million annually and take on average about 40 minutes of an adjudication staff member's time per claim (where the time estimate, again, includes clerical and supervisory time as well as interviewer time). The outcome of the adjudication interview is a determination of UI eligibility and associated benefits.[7]

---

[6] It should be noted that repetition of these steps is alleviated by telephone filing (see below) because phone interviews request all information needed to complete steps 1 and 2 during the same call, after which the computer system makes an automated decision about monetary eligibility for benefits.

[7] It is possible for claimants to appeal the results of determinations. Because appeals involve fairly specialized contention over UI rules and their application, we do not

4. All successful claimants are sent a continued claim form to complete and return by mail. The form requires responses to a number of standardized items (e.g., whether the claimant looked for work, received training, earned any money) as well as open-ended questions (e.g., job contacts made). It also asks claimants to sign a statement indicating that the answers they have given are true and that they are legally permitted to work in the United States.

5. These forms are scanned by optical character recognition (OCR) machines at one of two state claims centers. Data from the forms are then transferred over dedicated lines to the centralized UI database. The system also automatically generates the UI check and a stub that serves as the claimant's record of the transaction, along with the next biweekly continued claim form and a pre-addressed envelope for returning the form to the claim center.

These materials, in turn, are mailed to the claimant in a cycle that repeats steps 4 and 5 until the client has found work or has exhausted the eligibility period for UI benefits. Each biweekly claim takes a total of about 7 minutes of UI staff time to handle, on average.

6. Not surprisingly, clients have questions from time to time about the nature or status of the UI processes in which they are involved. These ad hoc queries (e.g., "When did you mail my second check?") are generally handled by UI customer-service representatives either at EDD's centralized call facilities or at a field office. In 1996, EDD's six centralized call facilities alone received over 8.6 million queries (because of a phased implementation plan, not all claimants in the state were served by call centers in 1996).

Procedures like those outlined here characterized all state employment security agencies until recently, when advances in telecommunications and computing technologies—coupled with the other pressures for change noted above—stimulated the exploration of alternative media for accomplishing UI program goals.

___

include them in our case study of individualized claims-related interactions with the UI program.

The chief drawbacks of traditionally conducted UI processes are that they are location dependent, time limited, and labor intensive. Moreover, they engage claims takers in routine data checking and data entry operations—tasks of far less value than activities such as delivery of job services. Consequently, EDD and other state employment security agencies have been investigating the potential of electronic avenues to improved program efficiency and effectiveness. We next review the opportunities to make use of e-mail to supplement current methods for carrying out individualized UI communications between EDD and its clients.

OPPORTUNITIES TO USE E-MAIL

EDD, as we have already noted, is looking toward new information and communication technologies to discover more-effective ways to meet the changing demands on its programs and services. To date, its UI-directed efforts are divided between Internet/Web-based systems and telephone-based systems.

Like all other state employment security agencies, EDD maintains a Web site that provides public information about its UI program (as well as other, related programs, such as job services). Additionally, like seven other state agencies, California's EDD provides Intranet applications for agency staff use.[8] However, aside from soliciting comments and suggestions about the Web site itself, EDD provides no mechanisms for official Internet-based "retail" communications between the UI program and its clients.

In contrast, telephone-based systems have been the focus of considerable planning, experimentation, and evaluation for handling two types of individualized communications in the UI program: ad hoc inquiries and initial claims. Of these two, telephone-based systems for answering client questions via automated interactive voice response (as a supplement to in-person response) are the more widespread and mature, having become operational statewide in 1997. Telephone filing of initial claims was introduced into one pilot site in Northern California's bay area in 1994; two more pilot sites became operational in 1995, one in San Diego and the other in Ven-

---

[8]See http://www.itsc.state.md.us/info/Internetapps/internetapps_sesas.html.

tura County. In 1997, all these telephone filing services were available via toll-free numbers, and by the end of June 1998, telephone-based initial claims filing was offered throughout the state. EDD believes that telephone filing will be the preferred system for initial UI claims (California Employment Development Department, 1996c). However, unlike the system that handles informational calls, this system relies exclusively on real-time in-person interaction with field office staff.

Nonmonetary determinations are handled, as before, by specially scheduled telephone interviews with adjudication staff. Continued claims, in contrast, are handled exclusively by mail. What potential benefits, then, might be associated with e-mail as a medium for managing any of these types of individualized interactions? The discussion below begins with ad hoc queries because they are comparable in many ways to queries handled by Medicare's ARUs (see Chapter Three). We then concentrate on interactions that go beyond exchange of individualized information to accomplish UI-related transactions.

Ad Hoc Inquiries

In EDD's UI program, calls for information are handled by customer-service representatives (CSRs) or by interactive voice response (IVR) units, in much the same way as customer-service functions are currently carried out by Medicare's fiscal intermediaries. An automatic call distributor, after eliciting the language preference of the caller (English, Spanish, other) and the nature of the query, places incoming calls into a queue pending the availability of an appropriate IVR unit or CSR.

At present, nearly all informational inquiries go to high-volume UI call centers (vs. local field offices). Among them, about a third are answered by IVR units. After obtaining some information from the caller for claimant authentication purposes, the IVR system retrieves the requested data from the centralized UI database and generates a voice response.

From EDD's perspective, relying on telephone centers to deal with informational calls offers a number of advantages over walk-in services or local calls to a field office. These include the ability to do fast and flexible load balancing and to improve call routing/redirection. Further, every call answered by an IVR unit directly reduces the time spent by CSRs on routine database lookup procedures. While clients also benefit from better load balancing and call (re)routing, a more salient advantage from their standpoint is access to customer services via IVR on a 24-hour seven-day-a-week (24/7) basis.

What added benefits, if any, could be gained by transferring these retail interactions to e-mail? It would be relatively unproblematic to create Internet and Web-based forms and procedures for handling the queries and responses now handled by IVR units. However, as the discussion of Medicare's ARUs points out, there is little to be gained by such a substitution. Instead, the greater potential benefits would come from the ability to decrease the proportion of queries that require real-time interaction with a CSR.

At present, the UI information made available through IVR units is very limited; they mainly provide the amount of a benefit check and the date of issuance. Other questions are referred to a CSR. In responding to them, however, the CSR relies on the same database that the IVR accesses. It is thus likely that an Internet/Web-based system—by providing a broader selection of well-formulated queries along with prompting, feedback, error detection/correction, and other capabilities not readily offered by a telephone interface— would permit claimants themselves to retrieve more of the information they seek. Further, it has been suggested that the ability to print computer-generated replies should reduce the number of repetitive calls—those made to re-ask particular questions because claimants have either forgotten parts of the answer and/or have not been able to write all of the information down correctly while the IVR was generating it.[9]

Informational calls not resolvable into well-formed database queries via an interactive and helpful interface would still need to be routed to an appropriate CSR for response, either by phone or e-mail. The preceding chapter discusses in some detail the drawbacks and advantages of free-form (vs. form-based) e-mail in comparison with

---

[9]Personal communication, Information Technology Support Center group interview, May 1997.

phone calls for handling Medicare customer-service functions. Many of the same points apply to UI customer-service queries.

In sum, the chief benefits to be gained from e-mail as a medium for handling UI customer-service queries lie in its disintermediation potential, reducing CSR time spent on routine database retrieval tasks while creating direct anytime/anyplace access to desired information for clients in multiple languages. However, the overriding conclusion to draw in the EDD case is that because informational calls account for a relatively small proportion of the total cost of individualized interactions between the UI program and its clients, the value of introducing e-mail as a supplement to customers' current query options is likewise relatively small. In what follows, therefore, we explore the potential role for e-mail in the three kinds of individualized UI communications that are transactional rather than exclusively informational in nature.

Initial Claims

In 1996, the focal calendar year for our data collection activities, just over 3,444,000 initial claims were filed with the UI program. Each claim required about 32.6 federal minutes-per-unit (MPUs) to complete, at an average cost of $9.70 each in field office staff time.[10] At these rates, the effort of handling initial UI claims as reflected in 1996 field staff time totaled about 896 person-years and cost over $33.3 million in 1996 field staff salaries.

Initial UI claims filing, then, represents a type of individualized interaction for which there could be significant savings of staff time and costs if e-mail filing could replace current procedures in a non-negligible number of cases (see Table 4.1).

Feasibility of Internet/Web filing. Internet/Web-based filing seems feasible for several reasons. First, according to EDD staff, 90 percent of initially filed claims are entirely routine. In these cases, comple-

---

[10] Federal minutes-per-unit are units of cost allocation for the state fiscal year. The cost is determined by multiplying the MPU by the average salary for a field office employee. This cost figure includes management and supervision in field offices, as well as time spent with claimants, but does not include operating equipment and expenses budgets.

Table 4.1

**Dollars and Person-Years Potentially Saved by Proportion
of Initial Claims Filed Electronically**

Percentage of Initial Claims Filed Electronically	Thousands of Dollars Saved	Person-Years Saved
10	3,338	90
20	6,676	179
30	10,015	269
40	13,353	358
50	16,691	448
60	20,029	538
70	23,368	627
80	26,706	717
90	30,044	807
100	33,382	896

tion of claims filing requires no special knowledge about UI procedures and can be carried out automatically once clients have provided their name, Social Security number, address, employer's name,
and other facts related to their ability to seek and accept work.
(Special handling is required for claims that include military service,
federal government, or out-of-state employer earnings, or that reflect
misreported Social Security numbers, wage discrepancies, or other
unusual situations that warrant further investigation.) Completing
all routine initial claims by e-mail would represent potential savings
of over 800 person-years annually in field staff time, or over $30 mil-
lion in 1996/97 fiscal year dollars.[11] Achieving even half the total
would reflect significant EDD gains (see Table 4.1).

Another feasibility-relevant consideration is that 60 to 70 percent of
initial UI claimants are repeat customers: They have filed claims
before. This means that most clients are familiar with filing procedures and that once client authentication has been assured, an In-
ternet/Web-based initial claim form could be presented to repeat
clients with a great deal of the requisite information already filled in.
Clients would need do no more than update some entries and/or

---

[11]Because the MPU includes clerical support as well as time spent by field
representatives interacting with clients, even the completion of all claims by e-mail
would not eliminate 100 percent of filing costs measured by MPUs.

make a few new entries before submitting the form. Even if we assume that among all routine initial claims, only the repeat claimants would be willing and able to file by e-mail, the result would nevertheless be a savings of 450 to 565 person-years annually in field staff time, or $17 to $21 million in 1996/97 fiscal year dollars. Again, reaching even half that goal would represent significant program savings (see Table 4.1).

Finally, feasibility is also suggested by the existence of models and precedents. In particular, ITSC, supported by the Department of Labor and housed at the University of Maryland, has developed a successful proof-of-concept prototype application and architecture for filing remote initial claims via the Internet/Web.[12] Two states, Maryland and North Carolina, have implemented Internet/Web-based systems for filing initial UI claims in specific facilities or under limited conditions; both states plan to expand the use of the medium. Eleven other states (California not among them) are planning such implementation projects.

E-mail and other options. Despite the feasibility of e-mail use for filing initial UI claims, EDD has concluded that telephony will be the medium of choice and has invested its planning, implementation, and evaluation efforts there. And, like Colorado, Massachusetts, and Wisconsin—all of which are also early adopters of telephone filing for initial UI claims—California makes data collected and lessons learned from its experiences readily available to others that are still involved in planning and decisionmaking about this alternative to in-person interactions (Information Technology Support Center, 1997). So any exploration of the potential role for e-mail in individualized UI interactions should take both in-person and telephone filing into account as other options.

---

[12]See ITSC Web site:

http://www.itsc.state.md.us/info/Internetapps/internetapps_sesas.html;
http://www.itsc.state.md.us/info/initial.html (Best Practices);
http://www.itsc.state.md.us/ITSC/inet/inetdemo.html (Demos);
http://www.itsc.state.md.us/ITSC/inet/inetclaims.html (Prototype); and
http://www.itsc.state.md.us/ITSC/delvrbles/Deliverables/P06/p06deli.html (Concept and Architecture).

It should be noted that these prototypes do not fully address issues of security, language barriers, and exception processing, all of which are major concerns for EDD.

Currently, many initial UI claims in California are still filed using telephones in EDD's local field office lobbies, even though toll-free telephone filing is available from other locations. This is because telephone filing of initial claims only became available on a state-wide basis in mid-1998 and is not yet widely known. However, varied outreach efforts have been under way since its initiation (California Employment Development Department, 1996d).

As mentioned earlier, EDD plans called for a total of six regional call centers statewide to handle all telephone filing. During 1996, when we began this study, telephone filing of initial claims was only available from three regional call centers. Clients could file initial claims from home or public telephones, but CSRs at local field offices also made (and continue to make) telephones there available for use (with their assistance) by walk-in clients willing to attempt filing by phone.

Operationally, phone filing works in very much the same way as traditional filing except that the claim is taken by a CSR over the telephone instead of in person. That is, the same centralized database supports the taking of claims by phone, with CSRs asking questions in real-time, entering new information into the database, using extant information for validation or verification purposes, helping clients to resolve inconsistencies, and so on. Changes to the system interface have been made, however, so that now CSRs are presented with easy-to-use data entry forms and carefully scripted questions for eliciting claimant responses (similar to computer-assisted telephone interviewing [CATI] screens). Additionally, call routing is provided. Queues have been established for filing claims in English and Spanish (the same as for IVR calls), as well as for federal, military, and interstate claims along with routine claims; within queues, load balancing across appropriate CSRs is also handled automatically by the system. Perhaps most important, initial claims can be completed without repeated callbacks.

Evaluations of these phone filing processes carried out independently by EDD and ITSC provide consistent evidence of a number of advantages over traditional filing. Client advantages include, most obviously, the convenience plus the time and cost savings of not having to travel to a field office to file a claim in person. Moreover, clients spend considerably less time filing claims. Clients interviewed in San Diego, for instance, indicated they spent an average of 124 minutes in the field office when filing an initial claim in person. The average time it took San Diego customers to file their initial claims by telephone was 13.4 minutes after reaching a CSR (Information Technology Support Center, 1997). Client perception and preference data likewise corroborate the success of these systems (see Table 4.2).

Advantages of telephone filing for initial UI claims to EDD thus far have to do chiefly with improved morale and safety. Because CSRs who take telephone claims no longer meet clients in person, EDD has dropped its dress code; casual clothing helps create a more comfortable and relaxed work environment. Greater employee safety has also been cited as an advantage for CSRs who work in call centers rather than field sites: Serving clients by phone has done much to reduce physical violence directed toward EDD field staff.

The greatest benefits to EDD from phone filing for initial UI claims lie in the future, however, when it will be possible to decrease the number of field sites to a small fraction of those that now exist. EDD's aim is to serve 90 percent of its UI customers remotely by the year 2000. Consolidating initial UI claims operations in a much smaller number of call centers will vastly reduce the cost to obtain and maintain physical facilities (plus associated overhead expenses).

Table 4.2

Client Response to Telephone Filing of Initial UI Claims
(percent)

1. Overall satisfaction with the telephone claim filing service

Site	Excellent	Good	Fair	Poor	Very Poor
San Diego	62	29	7	1	1
Ventura	63	25	8	0	3

2. Preference for method of claim filing

Site	Prefer Telephone	No Preference	Prefer In-Person
San Diego	93	5	2
Ventura	75	8	17

Further, it will allow for much greater leveraging of EDD's human resources, permitting one or a few staff to build special proficiencies in given UI functions (so that difficult or unusual cases of particular types can then be routed to those staff) while also facilitating cross-function staff shifts in the event of workload changes (e.g., due to mass layoffs, seasonality, or natural disasters). These capabilities, in turn, translate into service quality improvements.

The major cost advantages EDD will gain from telephone filing over traditional filing of initial UI claims, then, have to do with savings related to reductions in physical facilities, operating equipment, and associated expense budgets. A transition to remote Internet/Web-based initial claims filing would also yield these kinds of cost reductions, as well as the service improvements associated with leveraging of human resources, as described above.

Internet/Web-based initial claims filing, however, would potentially enable dramatic reductions in time spent by CSR staff on tasks that could be done by claimants (data entry) and by computers (database lookup, error detection and correction, prompting, feedback, and so on). Besides the labor time and cost reductions reflected in Table 4.1, above, such disintermediated procedures have the advantage of operating on a 24/7 self-service basis just as IVR queries do.[13] Further, the ability to offer Internet/Web-based initial claims forms readily in many languages could greatly relieve the need for live multilingual CSRs. In a polyglot state like California, where over 30 languages are represented among EDD claimants, this capability, too, could add significant advantages to e-mail filing.[14]

---

[13]Presently, the production database that supports initial claims filing is updated in real-time and is available to CSRs from 6:30 a.m. to 6:00 p.m. The IVR accesses a shadow file created from the production database once each evening; it is available on a 24/7 basis but not updated in real-time. Any claims that present a challenge needing CSR intervention would require a callback during normal business hours. The alternative—making CSRs available on a 24/7 basis—would have to be dealt with through collective bargaining processes because CSR-level jobs are not typically subject to shift work.

[14]Multiple languages present significant problems for EDD's remote filing services, given EDD's desire to serve all, on the one hand, and its level of resources, on the other. At this point, EDD offers claims filing services in English and Spanish in all areas; it offers services in Cantonese, Vietnamese, and TTY via dedicated 800-numbers; and its Operations Branch maintains a language resource directory to assist field staff in locating translators for other languages as needed.

Thus, the elimination of low-level CSR tasks now required for initial UI claims filing by phone and in person could permit reductions in staffing levels over time. More importantly, it could allow the redirection of CSR efforts to meet present-day demands for more intensive job services. Paradoxically, in periods of greatest unemployment (e.g., due to plant closings or peak seasonal layoffs), UI staff must dedicate most of their time to taking routine initial claims, leaving them least able to devote time to special job services when their customers most urgently need them.

In sum, there are significant advantages associated with e-mail filing of initial UI claims that cannot be attained by remote phone filing. Recognizing them, EDD had initially intended to offer both telephone- and Internet/Web-based options for filing initial claims (California Employment Development Department, Project Management Division, 1995). Why did it subsequently decide not to pursue the latter option? The answer is straightforward: access and equity differences. About 97 percent of U.S. households have at least one telephone. In contrast, less than 25 percent of the U.S. population has Internet access from either the workplace or their home, and those most likely to need UI services are among the least likely to have an Internet connection (U.S. Bureau of the Census, 1998; also see Chapter Six). Lack of near-universal access to Internet/Web technology, then, is viewed by EDD as precluding its ability to exploit the opportunities this medium affords for improving its services while reducing its costs. If such obstacles to e-mail filing for initial claims could be overcome, little extra cost and effort would be needed to make the medium also available for getting answers to routine informational questions. We return to this issue later in the report.

Continued Claims

In 1996, continued claims accounted for over 23,625,000 individualized interactions between clients and EDD's UI program. Each such claim took about 6.8 federal MPUs to complete, at an average cost of $2.03 in field office staff time. Although continued claim forms are short and require little staff attention, so many are filed annually that associated processing efforts represented nearly 1,300 person-years and cost over $47.9 million in 1996/97 field staff labor dollars.

Continued claims filing thus represents a subset of individualized UI transactions with an even greater potential for cost savings than initial claims filing if a substantial proportion of them could be carried out by e-mail (see Table 4.3).

Feasibility of Internet/Web filing. In principle, it would seem that the filing of continued claim forms via the Internet/Web is even more feasible than the filing of initial UI claims via that medium. First, regardless of how the initial claim is filed, current and correct data about claimants and their UI benefit eligibility are already in the centralized database; the new material to be entered for continued claim purposes is largely standardized and straightforward (California Employment Development Department, 1996b).

Further, after having completed initial filing by any medium, clients will have been told what to expect, so the continued claims process will find them at least partially prepared; and subsequent filings after the first continued claim will raise no new issues. At present, continued claim forms are typically completed by clients on their own and mailed in without assistance; they cannot be filed at walk-in field offices.

Table 4.3

**Dollars and Person-Years Potentially Saved by
Proportion of Continued Claims
Filed Electronically**

Percentage of Continued Claims Filed Electronically	Thousands of Dollars Saved	Person-Years Saved
10	4,790	129
20	9,581	257
30	14,371	386
40	19,162	514
50	23,952	643
60	28,743	772
70	33,533	900
80	38,323	1,029
90	43,114	1,157
100	47,904	1,286

Finally, feasibility is also suggested by the fact that data processing for continued claim forms is already automated—apart from scanning, the forms require virtually no human intervention. Many errors or inconsistencies might be caught by simple rules or filters at data entry time on a Web page, allowing flagging and correction during the same interactive session rather than requiring an additional effort. However, any remaining problems with the form, whether attributable to claimants or to OCR processes, could be handled as they are now; that is, they could generate an instruction to call a CSR to complete the claim. Anomalous on-line entries thus would likely be fewer in number and, in any case, would present no problems not already taken into account by standard operating procedures.

We pointed out earlier that 90 percent of all initial UI claims are routine and that 60 to 70 percent of these (or 54 to 63 percent of the total) are likely to be filed by repeat claimants. If all the repeat, routine claimants filed continued claims by e-mail, the savings to EDD would represent 700 to 800 person-years or more, or $25.8 to over $30 million in 1996 field staff costs. Again, achieving even half this rate of continued claims filing by e-mail would bring substantial gains to EDD compared to its present procedures (see Table 4.3).

E-Mail and other options. At present, use of paper-and-pencil forms and postal services is the only option for filing continued claims in California. However, it and several other states are exploring procedures for telephone filing of continued claims.[15] To date, only Nebraska has implemented Internet/Web-based forms for continued claims filing, although Maryland and North Carolina are also pursuing this alternative.[16] California will not give the Internet/Web serious attention as an option for continued claims filing, as would be expected, until access issues have been overcome (see Chapter Six for a detailed discussion of access to computers and networks in the United States). The remainder of the discussion in this section

---

[15]California's EDD recently tested technology for conducting continued claims certifications via touch-tone phone, assessing both the usability of the system and the accuracy of voice prints for security purposes. Based on the results, EDD is preparing a feasibility study for statewide implementation.

[16]See ITSC Web site: http://www.itsc.state.md.us/info/conclaim.html (Best Practices).

therefore considers advantages and disadvantages of the varied media options independent of access issues.

As explained earlier, in the discussion of Medicare's current paper-based procedures, relying on this medium is more costly than using e-mail for both the agency and the customer; and it is more costly for customers, although not necessarily for the agency, than is toll-free telephone service for accomplishing the same functions. Additionally, this medium's reliance on the U.S. Postal Service ("snail mail") is slower for completing transactions than either telephone or e-mail. Further, according to EDD, it is less reliable because of changes in address and insecurity of residential mailboxes. For these reasons, EDD hopes in the future to offer telephone filing as an alternative to postal filing procedures for continued claims. Presumably such an option could be implemented by relying only on IVR rather than in-person voice interactions.

There are, however, a number of advantages associated with the present method. First, postal service is at least as universal as telephone service and has already been consolidated into two large centers for purposes of processing continued claims. Thus, neither telephone nor e-mail methods would necessarily yield an advantage at the level of facilities acquisition and maintenance (although either or both would enable elimination of scanning staff time and OCR machines plus the problems associated with them). A second consideration is that UI benefit checks cannot at present be replaced with direct deposits. At least for the time being, then, EDD will incur the effort and cost of generating and mailing checks to its clients regardless of the medium in which continued claims transactions occur. (For security purposes, however, using different media for these purposes might be desirable.) Third, along with the check, the claimant receives paper-based documentation of the continued claims transaction from EDD (phone-based continued claims filing would not yield such documentation, while computer-based procedures would enable the printing of a paper trail).

For EDD, however, receiving paper-based documentation is even more important—especially for clients who have initially filed UI claims by telephone. Title 22 of the California State UI code, which originally specified that any person filing a claim must do so in person, was changed to pave the way for telephone filing. However, the

1986 Immigration Reform and Control Act still requires EDD to review the citizen or alien status of all UI claimants. The signatures on continued claim forms (captured in electronic media by OCR procedures) are taken to authenticate a client's status as a person legally entitled to work in the United States during the base wage period on which UI benefits are based as well as during the immediately prior two-week period covered by a particular continued claim.

A key element in the introduction of any advanced medium for continued claims filing, then, will be authentication procedures that provide the equivalent of a signed declaration. From EDD's perspective, phone filing would likely have to rely on biometric identifiers, such as voice prints, for authentication. Voice authentication is becoming more reliable technically, but it continues to present concerns because a sizable fraction of clients—especially those who do not speak English or who are hearing impaired—are likely to use surrogates (e.g., their children or other relatives or friends) to handle phone-based interactions with the UI program. E-mail procedures for continued claims filing would offer a broadened range of authentication approaches, although none of them has fully attained the recognized institutional status of a "signed original" (see also Chapter Five).

It should be underscored that EDD treats electronic documents (such as the electronic material created by CSRs based on client interviews) as official material of record.[17] Problems with authentication rather than with electronic media per se are what pose obstacles to telephone filing of continued claims from EDD's perspective. Could access issues be overcome, e-mail filing would face similar but probably less-severe authentication concerns.

Quite likely the greatest advantage that e-mail filing of continued claims would present over either the present method or a phone-based procedure is the opportunity to follow up on client responses to questions about jobs sought, training, and other work-related matters. While OCR procedures capture these short-answer responses, they do not do so in a way that can be made useful for profiling or job services purposes, either by human or computerized

---

[17]Personal communication, EDD Information Security Office interview, April 1997.

EDD agents. Providing the same information by means of an Internet/Web-based form would enable automated feedback and/or immediate linkage to job listings, training opportunities, and other relevant information and services. Clients would be able to get printouts not only of the filed claim for their records, but also of other advisory material provided. And EDD staff could retrieve and review the same material over time for individualized counseling purposes as appropriate.

Telephone filing could not be expected to yield the same advantages: a phone keypad, menu interface, and IVR together do not add up to the ability for clients to enter short answers of the sort described above or to receive the more extended material and further interaction options provided through Internet/Web linkages (e.g., connections to job banks). Such capabilities could be offered by phone, but only through extended real-time interaction with a CSR plus varied follow-ups and referrals. But besides the added cost to EDD of such an approach, clients would be restricted to using the system only during regular workday hours and would not leave the interaction with a printout of job search recommendations in hand.

We thus conclude that use of e-mail for filing continued UI claims could yield significant benefits to EDD and its clients. But such benefits can be attained only if problems of legal authentication (in addition to access problems) can be solved.

Nonmonetary Determinations

In 1996, more than 1,228,000 UI nonmonetary determinations were made by EDD adjudication staff members. As explained earlier, determinations of this nature are required whenever a claim (either initial or continued) raises complex questions about the claimant's eligibility for benefits. Although these determinations take longer to complete—40.2 federal MPUs, on average—than do either initial or continued claims, there are far fewer of them. Each nonmonetary determination cost about $11.95 to complete in 1996. Hence, on the basis of 1996 data, determinations represent about 394 person-years annually, or an expenditure of more than $14.6 million a year (see Table 4.4).

Table 4.4

Dollars and Person-Years Potentially Saved by Proportion of Determinations Completed Electronically

Percentage of Nonmonetary Determinations Completed Electronically	Thousands of Dollars Saved	Person-Years Saved
10	1,467	39
20	2,934	79
30	4,402	118
40	5,869	158
50	7,336	197
60	8,803	236
70	10,270	276
80	11,737	315
90	13,205	355
100	14,672	394

While nonmonetary determinations present a smaller target for cost savings than either initial or continued claims do, it is nonetheless worth exploring roles for Internet/Web-based media for these individualized interactions. First, although smaller, the potential for efficiency gains is still considerable. Second, looking only at the potential for cost savings does not take into account other kinds of benefits (e.g., opportunities to shift time to follow-up with clients or services and other performance improvements described above) that might, in the long run, do a great deal to improve program effectiveness. Third, nonmonetary determinations present challenges not fully represented by the other two types of individualized UI transactions.

Feasibility of Internet/Web determinations. Nonmonetary determinations raise feasibility challenges because they depend on special knowledge about UI regulations and procedures for their resolution. There is not a single set of brief objective questions which, when answered, automatically yield a correct eligibility determination. For this reason, whenever eligibility is in question, a telephone appointment is scheduled for the claimant with an adjudication staff member. The outcome of the adjudication interview is a positive or negative decision about eligibility status.

However, technologies presently available would support the presentation of eligibility-relevant queries to claimants in an interactive environment that accessed a rule system as well as the centralized UI database and prior claimant responses to generate next steps. The ensuing series of questions and answers would follow the logic of the rule system until either a determination was made or the claimant's case was referred to a human UI adjudication expert for determination.

The extent to which Internet/Web procedures can handle any of the individualized UI determinations now carried out via open-ended real-time interviews is not clear. The answer depends largely on how much of the reasoning about eligibility, as well as the application of relevant regulations to particular claimant cases, can be captured in a set of system rules. Researchers at ITSC, who are now in the process of developing such a rule system, believe that a substantial proportion of nonmonetary determinations could be made that way.

E-Mail and other options. Although e-mail is least promising both from a feasibility and a cost-savings standpoint, there are nonetheless a number of reasons for exploring it as a partial alternative to the present method for handling determinations. First, for the present process to work, a real-time interview has to be scheduled. In the past, claimants were simply given a specific date and time at which to call an adjudication center. This rigid procedure had to be replaced recently by more flexible scheduling, which is beneficial to clients but less manageable on EDD's side. An asynchronous procedure would be advantageous to EDD while permitting clients the greater convenience of a 24/7 adjudication service.

Second, given how the determination process is now carried out, even adjudication staff themselves would be likely to benefit from converting as much of their work as possible to a rule-based system. Currently, UI staff conducting eligibility determinations have, as data, hardcopy employer protests, claimant questionnaires, notes taken during interviews, and the like. Fact-finding guides and determination guides, available through a mainframe-based searchable text system, may also be brought to bear on the case at hand.

The cumbersomeness of this process has led EDD to explore the development of a "streamlined adjudication graphical environment"

(SAGE). If successful, the SAGE project is expected to accomplish a number of objectives: It will automate the fact-finding process, helping assure that all decision-relevant questions are asked of the parties involved; it will interact with the centralized UI database, presenting adjudication staff with all data pertinent to the client and the claim; and it will provide integrated access to manuals and guides. In the end, the system is expected to improve the quality of determination decisionmaking and its documentation (presently only the outcome of the adjudication decision, but nothing about the process itself, goes into the record).[18]

The sorts of efforts undertaken to develop a system such as SAGE could reasonably be expected to support the eventual development of a rule system and interactive interface usable by clients to proceed on their own as far as possible with the adjudication process. It is likely that no rule system will ever be complete, in part because the variation in individual cases is not entirely predictable and in part because the regulations or their interpretations are susceptible to change over time. However, if the more straightforward cases could be deferred to a rule-based interactive system, or if at least the initial parts of the interaction in more thorny cases could be so deferred, UI adjudication staff could focus their efforts on areas most in need of human expertise in eligibility determination.[19]

In sum, the use of e-mail to support complex individualized determination-related interactions offers enough potential advantages to be worth pursuing, at least as an adjunct to more labor-intensive adjudication interview procedures. Besides the issues of access and authentication discussed earlier, such procedures would likely also make questions about the legal status of official interactions carried out electronically more salient.

---

[18]See ITSC Web site, http://www.itsc.state.md.us/info/adjud/adjud.html (Best Practices).

[19]It would be interesting to learn whether the use of a rule-based interactive system to support adjudication could reduce the number of appeals, either because of improved routine decisionmaking and documentation or because of greater expertise available for making nonroutine determinations. If so, the cost savings potential would be greater than represented by the figures in Table 4.5.

E-Mail Opportunities Reviewed

We have shown that the three types of individualized communications associated with UI claim filing present different opportunities and issues. Table 4.5 clarifies the relative contribution of each type to the total cost of the field staff effort involved in claims processing. What it shows is that of the 2,576 person-years that annually go into claims processing, 50 percent of the total time is accounted for by the handling of continued claims, 35 percent by initial claims, and the remainder, by determinations. In other words, determinations—the type of individualized communication that would be the most difficult to convert to e-mail and that requires the most human expertise at present—account for the smallest proportion of total claims processing cost.

Provisionally, then, we conclude it would be well worth EDD's effort to attempt to develop Internet/Web-based systems for initial and continued claims processes if issues of access and authentication can be resolved. Creating a rule base to assist in handling determinations should be viewed as a longer-term aim; in the interim, however, progress toward this objective would likely prove helpful to adjudication staff. Further, all these efforts would also be likely to support the conversion of more ad hoc inquiries currently handled by CSRs in real-time into self-service e-mail queries to be answered automatically by interactions with the UI database.

Besides the potential for cost savings, a number of other advantages would be expected to result. First, the larger the proportion of individualized claims communications that can be handled by computer, the closer EDD comes to achieving its goal of giving clients di-

Table 4.5

Relative Contribution of Types of Individualized Communications to Total Savings in Descending Order of Importance
(percent)

Continued claims	50
Initial claims	35
Determinations	15
Total	100

rect access to its information and services—and doing so on a 24/7 basis. Second, having computers handle the more routine interactions would reduce the time claims takers spend on clerical activity (e.g., transcribing claimant data) and increase the time available for review, assessment, and decisionmaking. Even more important, it would permit staff to give much more attention to profiling, re-employment services, and related functions. In the long run, integration of UI program activities with improved job-related services could produce profound payoffs for the agency, its clients, and ultimately the state.

IMPLEMENTATION PROSPECTS AND CHALLENGES

In previous sections we addressed the possibilities associated with using e-mail for individualized claims-related communications. Here we discuss some of the implementation considerations that would have to be confronted.

Technological Constraints

Currently, the UI program relies heavily on a centralized hierarchical database that resides on a mainframe computer and is largely written in COBOL. Staff interact with this system, which takes care of most of the UI program's information and production needs, chiefly by means of character-based nonprogrammable 3270 terminals ("dumb" terminals) and leased data lines. Fire walls protect the internal database from access by users of the external database (e.g., callers using the IVR system).

These arrangements would require significant change to support the kinds of Internet/Web-based activities described above. First, while the legacy database could be retained on a mainframe computer, methods would have to be devised for other applications to interact with the mainframe system (at present the database does not permit standard relational queries, for example), probably through a decentralized client-server architecture. Second, network interoperability would have to be provided to permit Internet/Web-based communication with the system. Third, claimant applications would have to be developed to accomplish the functions now carried out by paper-based forms and UI staff interviewers, with a sufficiently friendly user interface to support self-filing.

Of these changes, the first two are already part of EDD's information technology strategic plan—and the last one, claimant software, would not necessarily require much more than the sort of software that claims takers themselves would prefer to use in a distributed system environment (California Employment Development Department, Information Technology Branch, 1996; California Employment Development Department, Project Management Division, 1996). Most organizations that still depend on legacy software, dedicated lines, and dumb terminals—whether in the public or the private sector—are contemplating similar kinds of changes simply because they can no longer afford to develop and maintain closed proprietary systems.

Security Challenges

Although technological changes of the kind outlined above would make the computer systems that support UI functions easier to use, maintain, and upgrade, they would also make them less secure. Any direct access systems, no matter how well protected, introduce new risks. However, EDD believes that continuing technical advances are enabling multiple approaches to system security (ranging from specialized chips and encryption software to fire walls and the secure sockets layer [SSL]) that are both reasonable to implement and acceptable from a risk management perspective. ITSC shares this view.

Already, according to EDD technical staff, experiences with encryption, personal identification numbers (PINs), and data cross-matching for verification purposes (in support of telephone filing) have provided the agency with valuable security lessons that will inform any move it makes toward Internet use (California Employment Development Department, 1996a).[20] Additionally, EDD has been systematically monitoring its payment data to determine whether rates of overpayment under telephone-filing conditions are

---

[20]EDD staff believe that the kinds of data cross-matching now undertaken for purposes of authenticating telephone claimants probably create greater security than did their former walk-in claims-filing procedures.

higher than historic rates. To date, these data, arrayed over time, show no discernible change in overpayment rates since the introduction of phone filing. However, staff in EDD's information security office believe they need stronger legal policy support. As an example, staff representatives mentioned the body of case law that protects individuals against wiretap—and the lack of comparable protection against "Internet tap."

As noted earlier, of the three aspects of security, authentication is perhaps EDD's strongest challenge. California law requires that individuals present proof of legal right to work before employment services can be provided. Unless digital procedures are developed to meet this challenge, continued UI claims will always incur the costs of some type of out-of-band communication.

Privacy also is a serious EDD concern. All data it receives from individuals are treated as private, according to EDD staff, although perhaps the most-sensitive data in the UI system are Social Security numbers and whatever data are linked to them. But wage history, health status (as might be indicated by a disability-related claim), and even litigation history (as might be indicated by determination appeals) are also sensitive; breaches of confidentiality, besides causing embarrassment, might negatively affect reemployment prospects. EDD staff say they are uncertain whether Internet communications pose more or fewer risks to privacy than ordinary telephone conversations do, apart from the lack of legal barriers to such privacy violations (discussed above).

Finally, there are system integrity worries. EDD believes it can protect its critical data for UI operations from intrusion once they reside in databases within the fire walls. But there are a number of possibilities (none of which have direct counterparts in the worlds of paper and telephony) for spoofing or gaming the kinds of systems that handle communications between external users and agency applications that could result in large-scale problems for the agency and/or its customers. For such potential security problems, timely surveillance of behavior throughout the networked system seems the most promising approach. Here, the need for timeliness, in particular, is emphasized; according to UI staff, it currently can take years—literally—before UI fraud is discovered.

As the discussion in Chapter Five emphasizes, government agencies at the federal and state levels face communication security challenges similar to these. It is unlikely—and probably undesirable— that a single solution be sought. But agencies should cooperate to develop a range of options to address their varied secure communication needs.

User Issues: Access, Equity, and Acceptability

Three key issues to address if clients are to use Internet/Web-based forms for self-filing of varied UI claims have to do with access, equity, and acceptability of e-mail. These are related issues, of course: If access to computers and networks were widespread in the UI claimant population, introducing e-mail as a medium for individualized communications with state agency services would not raise acceptability concerns. Or, if access were sparse in the UI claimant population but no different from access in the general population, e-mail filing would raise questions of acceptability but not of equity. However, as Table 4.6 shows, access to computers and networks is infrequent—and disproportionately so—among EDD's UI clients (U.S. Bureau of the Census, 1998).[21]

There are a number of reasons (related, for instance, to income and education level) why the UI claimant population is less likely than the general population to have access to computer and communica-

Table 4.6

Access to Computers and Networks by Employment Status
(percent)

	In the U.S. Population	In the UI Client Population
Access to a computer at home	43	31
Access to network services anywhere	22	13

NOTE: Data are from U.S. Bureau of the Census, 1998; methods used to generate table are explained in Chapter Six.

---

[21]See also Chapter Six.

tion technology (see Chapter Six for discussion). Another reason is that UI claimants are especially likely to have lost access to e-mail upon losing their jobs. A recent Bellcore report, noting a considerable "churn" in e-mail accounts, found that leaving a job was the most common reason people gave for no longer using e-mail (Katz and Aspden, 1997b). For such reasons, EDD decided against a pilot trial of the feasibility of e-mail use for initial claims filing. Its conclusion was that those most dependent on UI benefits would be least likely to benefit from this technological advance in service provision.

Could access and equity issues be resolved, there is no reason to think that acceptability would pose a formidable obstacle. Rather, virtually all scientific studies of the introduction of e-mail to diverse user groups (e.g., retirees, frail elderly, groups low in socioeconomic status) have found that once access barriers are overcome and training is provided, the medium is readily incorporated into day-to-day communication routines (Kraut et al., 1996; Hoffman and Novak, 1998; Bikson and Eveland, 1990; Bikson et al., 1991; Anderson et al., 1995, pp. 14–18). The National Research Council's 1997 report on every-citizen interfaces to the nation's information infrastructure supports this conclusion. It also suggests that advances in assistive technologies promise to make digital communication available to a broader range of individuals than can be served by any other medium (National Research Council, Computer Science and Telecommunications Board, 1997a).

Moreover, relying on today's graphical user interfaces together with well-designed forms, multiple response choices, partially completed entries, interactive coaching or prompting, error detection and correction, feedback, context-sensitive help, and the like might well lead to greater ease of use than is provided by the printed forms that still make up the bulk of individualized claims filed. Literacy studies indicate that UI claimants with the lowest levels of measured functional literacy remain unemployed the longest after an initial claim and thus file more continued claims than do their more literate counterparts (San Diego State University, Center for Learning, Instruction and Performance Technologies, 1996).

Such data suggest that presentation of information and elicitation of responses must be carefully designed to maximize understandability from the claimant's perspective, regardless of the medium (printed forms, phone interactions, or Internet/Web-based sessions). Further, applications that create effectively structured on-line interactions for self-filing of claims could, we believe, be provided with interfaces in the languages most commonly encountered among California's claimants. Such interfaces could be made more readily available, and potentially at reduced costs in the long run, than multilingual CSRs. At present, EDD is required to provide UI services in Spanish as well as in English. However, a 1996 survey of over 1 million UI clients in California indicated that thousands of EDD clients belonged to other language groups, including Vietnamese (4,851), Chinese (4,692), Tagalog (2,941), and Punjabi (1,444). In addition, Arabic, Armenian, Hindustani, Japanese, Korean, Portuguese, Samoan, and American Sign Language each accounted for over a hundred claimants.[22] As Chapter Two points out, the use of e-mail over other media in the conduct of official individual interactions could mean significant advantages for both agencies and their linguistically diverse clients.

Finally, implementation strategies would also make significant contributions to claimant acceptability. As noted earlier, even though most clients are familiar with telephony, phone filing for initial claims is being made available in walk-in field offices with CSRs on hand to help. E-mail filing might begin in the same way. ITSC, in fact, used this approach to test its on-line initial claims application software in a subset of field offices in Maryland. This strategy is viable only as long as walk-in field offices remain open. However, telephone hot lines could be made available to UI application users in need of help. Then, the user's location would not matter, as long as a phone was near the computer.

Another implementation strategy originally considered by EDD was to begin Internet/Web-based filing with clients at non-EDD sites where access and help would generally be available. For instance, about 8 percent of EDD's initial claims load is attributable to claims filed by applicants to California's county welfare departments for Medicare, Food Stamps, General Assistance, and Aid to Families with Dependent Children. Grant applicants must file a UI claim and no-

---

[22]These data come from the 1996 Dymally-Alatore survey of client language needs and were provided to RAND by EDD.

tify the cognizant welfare department of any UI benefit entitlement. Most welfare offices require customers to report in person to file these claims. Computers plus Internet/Web access to UI applications and help for self-filing could be made available at these sites. Such a procedure could result in a savings of over 70 person-years in CSR effort yearly, or about $2.67 million in 1996 salary dollars (see Table 4.1). Making the very conservative assumption that these individuals remain unemployed no longer than the average initial claimant, the continued claims savings would represent over 103 person-years in staff time, or over $3.8 million (see Table 4.2).

As another example, California's Worker Adjustment and Retraining Notification (WARN) Act of 1988 requires employers of 100 or more employees to notify the state Job Training Partnership Division when a plant closure affects either 50 or more of their employees or 33 percent of their active work force. In these cases, which account for over 1 percent of all initial claims filed, either the laid-off employees report to local EDD offices to file initial claims or arrangements are made for CSRs to go to the employer's facility to manage the filing process. The latter procedures incur additional expense but alleviate crowding and other load-related problems for EDD. Instead of sending CSRs, it would be fairly straightforward to make UI applications software available for use via the employer's computers and network connections. Not counting the extra costs of CSRs setting up off-site claims handling, e-mail filing of initial UI claims at the employer's facilities could save another 10 person-years of CSR time per year, or nearly one-half million dollars in wages. For continued claims, the savings would equal over 13 person-years and well over one-half million dollars annually.

Such starting steps would provide EDD with valuable experience for enhancing the acceptability and ease of use of e-mail filing. At the same time, increasing availability of Internet/Web facilities in libraries and other community settings will also help bridge the access gap. It is also worth considering whether the kinds of cost savings represented by EDD's potential gains from handling individualized interactions by e-mail, when multiplied by the hundreds of government functions with which U.S. citizens need to interact, might not offset expenses incurred in defraying Internet costs to fully address the equity challenge.

Organizational Innovation

We began this chapter with a discussion of the pressures on EDD for change, ranging from a greater number of expected unemployment episodes per person (because of technological change as well as changes in industry employment practices) to a stronger push for linking UI programs to job services (e.g., because of welfare-to-work legislation). These pressures, combined with demands to streamline agency budgets while retaining high quality in state government services, have helped to stimulate agency exploration of networked information media. Thus far, as apparent in the foregoing discussion, these explorations have mainly examined the ways in which advances in telecommunications technologies could substitute for current operations.

Studies done at RAND and elsewhere converge on redesign of business processes as the right starting point for addressing questions of how to improve services using new information and communication technologies. To avoid simply automating current flows of work, institutions are advised to begin by analyzing their activities in terms of a cascade of objectives from basic missions to the primary processes that make up those missions. Because of many characteristics unique to governmental missions, however, agencies cannot wholly embrace the "obliteration" model of reengineering that many commercial firms have been advised to adopt.

Rather, an intermediate approach is needed, one in which information objects, including form-based and free-form communications (whether carried out by e-mail or telephone), are construed as primary process intermediaries; that is, they should be seen as having instrumental roles in the accomplishment of business missions. As EDD and other agencies define and analyze new demands on their business processes, they may determine that current boundaries between organizational units and/or between program-defined information flows (e.g., UI vs. job services) are creating impediments to more-effective mission performance. In such cases, they may undertake to restructure intra- or interorganizational relationships, or combinations of these, in ways that take existing technologies and political realities into account. Even for-profit firms have come to realize that old-style reengineering-oriented analyses have often failed because they overlook the nonroutine nature of knowledge-based service processes as well as the tacit, contextual basis of many effective business practices.

For these reasons, our EDD case study relies on an "as-is" model of business processes and attempts to demonstrate the potential cost savings for current operations that could come from replacing varied types of in-person interactions with Internet/Web-based communications. We did not consider potential savings associated with reducing the number of field offices maintained, since advanced uses of telephony could presumably yield similar savings. Further, we dramatically underestimated the potential societal gains that might come from redeploying at least some of EDD's human resources—now dedicated to UI activities—to the job services area. And we ignored the expected societal value of service integration across agencies that might derive, for example, from linking job services/UI activities with welfare-to-work efforts carried out by the Department of Social Services. However, moving current operations on-line would do a great deal to facilitate such major business process design improvements.

Chapter Five

SECURITY AND RELATED TECHNICAL ISSUES[1]

The case studies presented in the previous two chapters highlight the fact that much (but certainly not all) of the communication between governments and individual citizens may involve the transmission of sensitive information. The full potential of these new media will not be realized until means are developed for secure interactions.

Technology to support secure communication exists today. Similarly, the physical and commercial infrastructure for widespread digital communication—the public switched network, ISPs, and similar components—already exists or is being built. What does not exist, however, and does not appear to be imminent, is the institutional, legal, organizational, and administrative infrastructure to support a potentially universal (i.e., available to any citizen who wants it) system for secure and binding e-mail communication between government agencies and individual citizens. We describe here those institutional, organizational, and administrative issues that must be addressed and overcome to achieve workable secure communication between government and citizens, mention some

---

[1]On November 6 and 7, 1997, with the sponsorship of The Markle Foundation, RAND convened a workshop in Washington, D.C., addressing the character of the required security infrastructure for government-citizen communication, who might plausibly provide it, how it might be financed, and what other policy changes—institutional, legal, programmatic—might be necessary. Attendees at the workshop included managers, policymakers, and analysts from a variety of government agencies at the state and federal level and representatives of private-sector concerns that are users or providers, current or potential, of secure communication services. This chapter is based primarily on the results of that workshop, which are also described in Neu, Anderson, and Bikson, 1998.

government initiatives under way, and then address some other related issues that are primarily technical in nature.

NEED FOR SECURE COMMUNICATION

As previous chapters indicate, many government communications with individual citizens involve the transmission of such sensitive information as tax forms, records of health care, and transactions involving entitlement to government benefits. In some cases, communications between citizens and government agencies are also legally binding (tax returns, for example). Consequently, some electronic communications between government agencies and individual citizens will have to be highly secure.

What do we mean by "secure"? A secure system requires four main elements:[2]

- *Authentication.* Ensure that transmissions and messages, and their originators, are authentic, and that a recipient is eligible to receive specific categories of information.

- *Data integrity.* Ensure that data are unchanged from their source and have not been accidentally or maliciously altered.

- *Nonrepudiation.* Ensure that strong and substantial evidence is available to the sender of data that the data have been delivered (with the cooperation of the recipient), and, to the recipient, of the sender's identity, sufficient to prevent either from successfully denying having sent or received the data. This includes the ability of a third party to verify the integrity and origin of the data.

- *Confidentiality.* Ensure that information can be read only by authorized entities.[3]

---

[2]These categories and their definitions are taken from Federal Public Key Infrastructure Steering Committee, 1998.

[3]The importance the public attaches to confidentiality and privacy was illustrated in April 1997 by the outcry against and the subsequent discontinuance of a service offered by the Social Security Administration that allowed citizens to have immediate access via the World Wide Web to individualized Personal Earnings and Benefit Estimate Statements (PEBESs). Even though the information required for on-line

Some electronic communications between government agencies and citizens will likely require more stringent protections than do traditional paper-based or in-person transactions. The scale and velocity of traditional transactions are limited by the very nature of these transactions: Requests for information have to be submitted, information copied and mailed, and so forth. Breaches of security are likely to affect one citizen at a time. But as databases of sensitive information become increasingly accessible on-line, the consequences of a security failure may multiply. Rather than stealing a single SSN or credit-card number, a determined, skilled, and criminally inclined hacker might succeed in gaining access to files that contain identifying information for thousands of individuals. The same ease of access that makes electronic access to databases attractive in the first place could permit a malefactor to download large amounts of sensitive information or carry out hundreds of illegal transactions in seconds—much too quickly, perhaps, for authorities to recognize or to plug a breach.

Of course, nongovernmental users of electronic communications also require confidentiality, integrity, nonrepudiation, and authentication (in pursuing, for example, on-line commercial transactions). And some kinds of nongovernmental communication (the transmission of medical records, for example) may involve information as sensitive as anything kept in government files. Systems for secure e-mail communication are already being developed to serve the needs of these nongovernmental users. Government agencies may be able simply to piggyback on this infrastructure, and it would certainly be wasteful to create a parallel infrastructure purely for government purposes. Ideally, a common infrastructure (but not necessarily a single, integrated, hierarchical *system*) for secure governmental and nongovernmental e-mail communications will emerge.

But there is no guarantee that a secure communication infrastructure developed for commercial purposes will be suitable for government-related uses. In particular, there is no guarantee that privately

---

access—name, SSN, date of birth, and mother's maiden name—was the same information required for in-person or postal access, many saw electronic transmission of Social Security–related information as insufficiently secure and open to potential abuse.

developed systems will provide the potential for universal access that must be a key feature of systems meant to facilitate government-citizen communication. At the very least, government agencies will have to articulate—sooner rather than later—their needs for security and undertake assessments of the degree to which independently developed approaches satisfy those needs.

Government agencies might also play a useful role in promulgating security standards that can then be widely adopted by nongovern-mental users. (The U.S. Department of Health and Human Services, for example, has already established standards for the electronic transmission of personal medical information.) And, above all, gov-ernment agencies will have to create a general policy environment that will encourage the development of secure and binding e-mail communications for all purposes.

ELEMENTS OF SECURE COMMUNICATION

Consider first the diagram of the elements of citizen-government communication shown in Figure 5.1. This figure simplifies many as-pects of the communication: The citizen will likely use an ISP or a business computer that maintains his or her e-mail account. The government agency will have a "gateway" computer maintaining its link to the Internet, with a number of computers, networks, databases, servers, and so forth linked to that gateway machine. For our purposes, however, Figure 5.1 shows the essential elements.

RAND *MR1095-5.1*

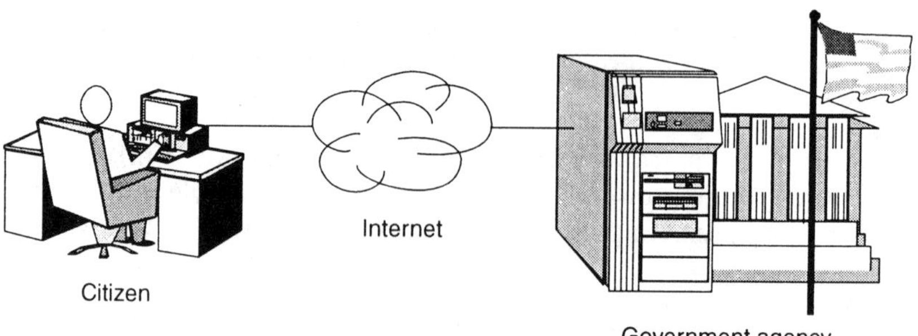

Citizen

Internet

Government agency

Figure 5.1—Citizen-Government Communication

Consider now the four elements of security mentioned above: authentication, data integrity, nonrepudiation, and confidentiality.

Citizens type an e-mail message on their PCs, or one is created through interactions with a World Wide Web page provided by the agency, accessed (i.e., downloaded to the PC) for the purposes of that interaction. *Confidentiality* of that message can be assured *as it passes over the communication links and the Internet* through the use of encryption generated within the PC, and the encrypted message can then be unscrambled within the agency's recipient machine. Note the italicized phrase above. The message may well remain unencrypted when stored within the citizen's PC disk files and after decrypting within an agency computer. Additional privacy can be obtained through encryption of those files also, if the greater expense of time and trouble is deemed merited by either or both of the participants.

In this simple case, we have provided *link encryption:* privacy of the contents of the message as it traverses the various communication links between the citizen's PC and the agency computer. Three current popular ways of providing link encryption are use of the secure multipurpose Internet mail extensions (S-MIME) protocol, the secure sockets layer (SSL) protocol built into most Web browsers, and a public key infrastructure (PKI) in which digital "certificates" are created and exchanged to verify the identity of and various authorizations granted to an individual or an agency. (More on such certificates, and certificate authorities, below.)

In short, for citizen-government communication privacy purposes, link encryption would suffice, and standard software packages providing S-MIME or SSL protocols could provide the necessary transmission security, most often transparently and silently without requiring user knowledge or intervention.[4]

---

[4]We do not dwell here on secure storage of files—be they paper or electronic—within government agencies. File storage security is an important topic (especially when bulk abuses of electronic files are possible) but is beyond the scope of this discussion. The reader should keep in mind, however, that the real risk may lie more in access— perhaps illicit bulk, wholesale access—to electronic file systems (on government computers; on personal PCs) than in the transmission of transactions across telephone lines or the Internet.

Similarly, the *integrity* of a message as it proceeds from a citizen's PC to a government computer is quite easily provided. A mathematical function representing the content of a message can be embedded in the message and encrypted; when the message is received and decrypted, that same function is calculated on the received message to verify that it matches the original function.

So confidentiality and integrity can be maintained, usually without human involvement or intervention, between a citizen's PC and an agency's computer. Most Web browsers and e-mail software packages contain the relevant protocols and processing, waiting to be invoked.

What about *authentication* and *nonrepudiation*? How can a valid government agency assure that it is communicating with a particular citizen—and vice versa—and in a manner that leaves a sufficient and reliable audit trail of the interaction? This task is more difficult, for the following reasons:

- Some cryptographic systems, such as the SSL scheme used by popular Web browsers, operate "in the background" without any user intervention or special knowledge. Thus, by sitting down at person B's machine, person A can mimic person B for any systems that rely on the identity of the computer to identify the individual user. The only remaining form of security (assuming there is no fingerprint reader, retinal scanner, or other biometric device attached, and no required use of an auxiliary physical "token" such as a "smart card" with embedded memory and logic) would be interactions between a government agency and citizens querying for data known only to them—the usual ritual of mother's maiden name and SSN. But these facts are widely known by other family members and are increasingly accessible in databases, such as motor vehicle department records, or even on drivers' licenses.

- Other, more elaborate encryption schemes, most notably those employing a PKI, rely on each user possessing one or more key pairs, each comprising a "public" key known to his or her correspondents and a "private" key known only to the user. Yet these keys are complex strings of digits (bits) that will not be memorized and typed by users; they are usually stored in files[5] on a user's PC and are protected by a simple password (usually comprising eight characters or fewer) that is often something rather easily guessed—the name of the user's pet dog or cat, a child's nickname, a license plate number. So all the elaborate encryption that represents both the identity of and the authorizations granted to a user could be unlocked with a simple password, given access to a user's PC. "Identity theft" may be as simple as guessing a password.

There are solutions to the above problems, but they most often involve, as mentioned earlier, use of some physical "token," such as a smart card—i.e., a credit-card-like device containing a built-in computer chip and memory.

In short, elaborate and secure encryption schemes can provide sufficient protection to ensure confidentiality and integrity of messages as they are transmitted between a citizen's computer and a government's computer, or vice versa. Authentication of the individual or government agency and nonrepudiation are more difficult to achieve, and might founder on the fact that complex keys enabling such schemes are often saved under a simple password the user must memorize (and that therefore often relates, for mnemonic purposes, to details in that user's life). Authentication can also be achieved through a query-response process invoking details of the user's life that only he or she should know—but that are increasingly known to others in today's data-based society.

Such measures are incomplete. But they are also incomplete for other means of communication, such as postal mail. Like security measures for postal mail, those for electronic transactions must be augmented by laws and regulations against misuse (the goal being to dissuade those who would tamper with or misuse this communication medium) and that provide punishment for those who take advantage of security weaknesses. As with so many other real-world problems, the main emphasis must be placed on risk management, as so eloquently stated in a November 1998 speech by Daniel E. Geer,

---

[5]These files are called by some software programs a "digital wallet" or some such evocative phrase.

Jr. (Geer, 1998). And any risk management assessment must especially take into account perhaps the greatest continuing security risk in information systems: trusted insiders that abuse their privileges.

Given these complications and caveats, many observers still believe that a PKI is the basis on which widespread secure communication, involving both authentication of the identity of the communicator and the various authorities allowed to that person (e.g., for information access or modification), may be evolved on a large scale in our society. We next present a brief overview of the ideas and concepts underlying public key encryption and PKI.

PUBLIC KEY ENCRYPTION AND INFRASTRUCTURE

Today, arrangements for secure digital communications often employ some form of public key encryption (PKE).[6] In such systems, each user has one or more key pairs: a public key known to the user's correspondents and a private key known only to the user. These keys can be used in either of two ways: as encryption keys, to ensure the confidentiality of messages, or as signing keys, to confirm the identity of the sender.

When a correspondent encrypts a message with the intended recipient's public key, the message can be read (decrypted) only by the intended recipient using his or her private key. Similarly, if the correspondent "signs" the message using his or her private key, the recipient can use the correspondent's public key to check the signature and confirm that the message came from the named correspondent. By attesting to the origin and integrity of an electronic document, such "digital signatures" may, in appropriate circumstances, make the document binding on the sender (many states have enacted laws making digital signatures that meet certain standards the legal equivalent of traditional physical signatures).

At the heart of a large-scale PKI system are one or more so-called certificate authorities (CAs)—trusted institutions or organizations that "certify" that a particular public key is associated with a particular user. In essence, a CA establishes an electronic identity for each user

---

[6]For one of many introductions to PKE, see National Research Council, 1996.

of its services. For others to have confidence in this identity, a CA must also be able to provide nearly instantaneous verification that a particular user/public key pairing is still valid—i.e., that the user or other authority has not for some reason canceled a public key.[7] Usually, a CA will demand proof of identity (perhaps a driver's license, birth certificate, passport, or application form bearing a notarized signature) before issuing a digital certificate binding the public key to the user.[8] Typically, a CA will also provide customer services, such as replacing certificates that have been lost or compromised, publishing directories of public keys, and assisting users who experience difficulties.

Identity vs. Authority

By associating a public key with a particular user, the CA establishes the electronic *identity* of that user. To complete a system for secure communication, a government agency or commercial institution must grant this user, whose identity can now be verified, *authority* to access information, to make use of services, to carry out transactions, etc. The act of establishing authority will typically require additional measures beyond those necessary to establish identity. For authorization purposes, for example, a particular electronic identity may need to be associated with particular accounts or records that the user is allowed to access.

Authorization—associating electronic identities with specific records or accounts—may be performed directly by the agency or institution granting access to records or accounts. Although an organization or agency must retain the responsibility for establishing identities or authorities, it may contract out to a third party the processing of electronic records that keep track of those certifications. The organizations with responsibility for granting authorities are commonly (perhaps confusingly) called certification authorities, because they certify the right of particular individuals to access particular files or

---

[7]If a private key is lost or compromised, a user must replace both the public and the private key.

[8]Some CAs issue different kinds or levels of certificates, depending on the kind of supporting identifying materials required.

services. Current usage distinguishes between *identity certificates* and *authority certificates.*

The two functions—establishing identity and establishing authority—are distinct and quite separable. A CA issues an identity certificate asserting that a particular electronic identity is associated with a particular user. If a government agency or commercial institution accepts this assertion—i.e., believes that the CA did an adequate job of verifying the user's identity—it may then issue an authority certificate granting that user authority to execute specific transactions (for example, accessing a Social Security file or a bank account, filing an application or tax return, placing an order, or registering a motor vehicle). Some CAs may both certify identities and authorize transactions within specified domains, but this combination is neither necessary nor necessarily efficient. Indeed, the processes required to issue the two kinds of certificates are likely to be quite different. Identity certification will typically require some direct, perhaps in-person, interaction with individual users. Authority certification will typically require routine processing of large databases and updating of links between electronic identities and particular accounts or records.

An individual user may have more than one electronic identity, and each such identity may be granted multiple authorities. For example, one person may have the identity "Trustee of John Doe Trust with certain authorities granted thereto" (for example, authority to initiate specified financial transactions) and the identity "staff member of the XYZ Corporation" with other authorities (say, building access or purchasing authority). The CA that establishes identity does not need to know what specific authorizations a particular person has been granted or had revoked. If the CA granting authorization relies on another CA to establish identity, a trust relationship based on clearly understood standards and accountability must be put into place and maintained between the two CAs. In some cases, authorization may not require identification in any absolute sense. A merchant may, for example, authorize a purchase knowing the credit card or bank account to be charged but not the personal identity of the buyer. For most sensitive government-related transactions, however, it seems likely that personal identity will have to be clearly established before authorizations are granted, and any government agency relying on other CAs to establish identity will need to be linked to those other CAs by a well-established "web of trust."

Who Can Act as Certificate Authorities for Government Agencies?

Widespread and versatile communication between government agencies and citizens will depend on a CA or group of CAs that can meet the following criteria:

- *Highly reliable identification of agencies and users.* The government activities that generate the highest volumes of individualized communications often require the transmission of extremely sensitive information. Government agencies and citizens will require a very high degree of confidence that they are in fact each communicating with the intended party.

- *Local presence.* To ensure reliable identification of users, CAs may require in-person interactions and perhaps the physical presentation of certain documents. This in-person interaction may have to be repeated periodically to maintain the validity of the digital certificate. If secure electronic communication is to be available to any citizen who desires it, then every citizen (e.g., within a city or a state, or within the entire United States for federal government applications) will have to have easy access to an office of a suitable CA.

- *Extensive customer service.* A system that allows secure electronic communication with government agencies for any citizen who desires it will require a robust customer service operation— to answer questions, guide infrequent and perhaps unsophisticated users, and restore or replace lost or compromised certificates.

Although increased use of e-mail communication could result in significant cost savings for government agencies, it is unlikely that these savings would be large enough to justify the considerable expenses associated with any single agency's acting as a CA—especially as an identity CA—solely to support its own communications. And citizens would not be well served if they had to establish different electronic identities for every government agency they wished to deal with. If secure communication between government agencies and citizens is to become commonplace, therefore, some organization(s) will have to provide CA services that make communications possible with multiple government organizations.[9] Ideally, electronic identities provided by these CAs would also be useful for commercial or nongovernmental communications.   But who will provide these communication services?[10]

A variety of private sector actors may be well positioned to provide CA services for secure communications between government agencies and citizens. In recent years, a number of *specialist firms* have begun to offer CA services. VeriSign, GTE Cybertrust Solutions, Digital Signatures Trust Company, and Cylink are some of the early entrants into this market. Although all of these firms hope for future growth, all still serve relatively small and specialized populations. Whether they can or wish to expand their operations to the entire population—including many users who might require extensive customer service and may not generate much revenue—remains to be seen. Also open to question is whether CA firms oriented (at least today) primarily toward facilitating private commercial transactions will find it worthwhile to meet possibly specialized standards of identification certainty and authorization control required for citizen-government communication.   Similarly open to question is whether citizens will wish to entrust the security of sensitive government-related transactions to commercial firms.

Banks may be well placed to provide CA services for government-citizen communication. They have ongoing trusted relationships

---

[9]In fact, the Federal Public Key Infrastructure Steering Committee is wrestling with these issues. (See http://www.gits-sec.treas.gov for details.) This committee is also developing a "Bridge" facility allowing separate PKI systems within the federal government to share certificates and trusted relationships. Initiatives for establishing a PKI are also being taken within the Internal Revenue Service and the Department of Defense ("IRS Award Assists Firm in Bid for DoD PKI," *Defense Information and Electronics Report*, September 11, 1998). In particular, the latter is now implementing a "medium" level PKI system potentially used by millions of persons for access to and transmission of sensitive but unclassified information. (See http://www.disa.mil/infosec/pki-int.html.)

[10]Identifying suitable providers of CA services for interactions with the government is not of purely theoretical interest. The General Services Administration of the federal government has prepared a draft request for proposals for a "pilot demonstration" to provide CA services for a broad range of federal agencies.

with their customers and already go to some lengths to establish customers' identities. (It is a legal requirement in banking to "know your customer.") Banks have many points of presence in almost all communities and, at least occasionally, deal face-to-face with their customers. The movement toward direct deposit of government benefits means that even low-income Americans are increasingly likely to have bank accounts and to be in routine contact with a bank. Banks are familiar with needs for data security, authenticity, and privacy. Moreover, they are already closely regulated, and the extension of this regulation to include standards for identifying customers and universal access may not be a large step. Banks are also in the business of risk management, into which security issues ultimately devolve (Geer, 1998). Finally, many banks are moving toward creating electronic banking systems to serve their customers. It may turn out that such bank infrastructures can be exploited for communications with the government at minimal additional cost.[11]

Other institutions that maintain continuing relationships with individual citizens might also be able to provide CA services. Consider, for example, large *health insurance providers* or *health maintenance organizations.* Such organizations routinely establish basic identity information on their members and patients. Increasingly, these organizations may desire to communicate sensitive information (diagnostic test results, payment information, appointment verifications, etc.) to doctors and patients electronically, and they may develop secure communication systems for their own purposes. Electronic identities established for these purposes might be sufficiently reliable for the transmission of sensitive government information. Indeed, the federal government is already drafting security standards for the electronic transmission of health-related information. These organizations also have legitimate needs for information relating to some government programs (Medicare, Medicaid, and Social Security), and extending their on-line communication systems to allow direct citizen-government interaction may be a natural step.

---

[11]In January 1998, the Office of the Comptroller of the Currency granted permission for the first time for a bank to provide CA services. A subsidiary of Zions Bank, Digital Signatures Trust Company, is issuing digital certificates to facilitate electronic filing of legal documents. (See Office of the Comptroller of the Currency News Release NR 98-4, January 13, 1998.)

In carrying out their missions, some government agencies and quasi-governmental entities have frequent or regular interactions with large numbers of citizens. They may, therefore, be plausible candidates for providing CA services to a broad population.

The *Social Security Administration* (SSA), for example, has a nationwide system for creating a kind of digital identity—the SSN—that is already widely used to verify many kinds of transactions. Upgrading the SSN to a public/private key pair is perhaps not too farfetched to be considered, although there has been resistance in the past to allowing the SSN to become anything resembling a national identification number. The issuance of SSNs does not currently meet the standards for identity verification we have described for digital identity certificates by CAs.

The *U.S. Postal Service* (USPS) maintains a relationship with every address in the country (if not, strictly, with every individual), and most Americans live within a short distance of a post office. Government agencies and individual citizens have grown accustomed to entrusting confidential materials to USPS for delivery. Over the years, a substantial body of law and regulation has created a special status for postal mail. USPS is not liable, for example, for losses suffered because a letter is not delivered. Tampering with mail and using the mail to perpetrate fraud are federal offenses, and postal inspectors "with badges and guns" are empowered to deal with offenders. E-mail, of course, enjoys no such protections today, but many see the extension of at least some postal regulations to e-mail as useful in the maturation of the new medium. This extension might prove more natural or graceful if USPS were chosen to manage a system for secure e-mail.

Finally, state *departments of motor vehicles* may deserve some consideration as CAs. After all, they issue the most commonly used means of identification in America today—drivers' licenses. Most also issue identification documents to nondrivers. Why not, some ask, extend this identification service to the electronic realm?

One CA or Many?

Most government agencies communicating via e-mail (and most private firms, for that matter) will necessarily maintain unique processes for granting and verifying access authorizations. Although they may contract with other agencies or outside firms for the actual authorization, they will establish authorization and access policies specific to their own requirements. HCFA, for example, will presumably not rely on the SSA or the IRS, much less some private firm, to determine who will have access to a citizen's medical information.

But there is no reason for different government agencies to maintain their own procedures or to rely on different CAs to establish the identities of electronic correspondents. Indeed, life will be simpler for citizens if many government agencies can agree to accept identity certifications from a common set of CAs. One pair of public and private keys would work for government transactions with different agencies. Ideally, identities established for government purposes would also suffice for nongovernmental commercial or financial transactions. A single digital signature would be adequate for multiple purposes, just as a single physical signature is today.

This does not imply, however, that a single CA must or should provide identity certificates for all citizens. If several CAs (perhaps a number of private firms specializing in CA services, a number of banks, and USPS) all provided identification services that met established government standards for reliability and validity, there is no obvious reason why citizens should not be allowed to choose the CA whose services they found most convenient or attractive, just as consumers are now free to choose among long-distance telephone carriers and ISPs. Competition among CAs might help to constrain the price of CA services and to maintain the quality of their customer service. Being deemed acceptable for communications with government agencies could be a valuable selling point for CA providers; a bank, for example, might attract customers to its on-line banking services by advertising that the same digital key that provides access to checking account balances is also accepted by HCFA should a customer want to check on the status of a Medicare claim.

A choice among CA providers may also alleviate concerns among some citizens about the creation of a monolithic "big brother" capable of observing or monitoring all of a citizen's e-mail transactions. A citizen who feels more comfortable using one key to file tax returns, another to respond to census inquiries, and yet another to facilitate personal banking transactions, and who is willing to put up with the inconvenience associated with establishing and managing multiple keys, might welcome the existence of multiple providers of CA services.[12]

SOME SECURITY-RELATED ISSUES TO BE RESOLVED

Along the path to an infrastructure for routine, secure e-mail communication between government agencies and individual citizens, a number of potentially difficult policy issues will have to be dealt with.

Responsibilities of CAs. In essence, a CA certifies that a particular public key is associated with a particular individual or authorization and has not been canceled or compromised. What happens if the CA gets it wrong or assigns keys to an impostor? Almost certainly, CAs must bear some legal or financial responsibility if communications are compromised because of their failures. Contracts offered by commercial CA firms today typically spell out in considerable detail the limits of the CA's liabilities in various circumstances. But no standards exist for such terms and conditions,[13] including a statement of which protections are adequate for communications involving government agencies. What sanctions will be applied in case of a security breach? And if a CA complies with government guidelines for verifying identity, can the CA be held accountable for subsequent lapses?

Managing and protecting private keys. Exactly how individual citizens will create, record, protect, and use their private keys has not yet been clearly worked out. As mentioned earlier, these keys will be

---

[12]Apparently, existing legal restrictions on the actions of government agencies and assurances that information will not be inappropriately shared between government agencies are not sufficient in the view of some citizens. A representative from the IRS told us that many taxpayers resist providing the IRS with bank account numbers for the direct deposit of income tax refunds. Very stringent legal restrictions on IRS activities notwithstanding, these taxpayers apparently fear that providing information on their bank accounts might allow IRS personnel to pursue improper investigations of their financial activities.

[13]However, a task force on certification authority rating and trust, under the auspices of the Internet Council of the National Automated Clearing House Association (NACHA), is developing policies to allow government agencies to evaluate the reliability, trustworthiness, and performance of CAs. Representatives from state and federal government agencies, as well as from the private sector, are participating. (See http://internetcouncil.nacha.org.)

long strings of digits, impossible for anyone to remember, and users will need some repository ("digital wallets") for their keys. A convenient solution would be for users to store keys in password-protected files on their PCs. A user (or the application program) would simply choose the appropriate key for any transaction, with the user activating the key by typing an easily remembered password. But there are dangers in storing encryption keys on PCs. In an increasingly networked world, it is too easy for someone else to read even supposedly protected files. And what about occasions when keys are to be used away from the user's home computer?

The legal status of electronic transactions. There is widespread recognition that laws have not kept pace with technology in regard to digital communication. E-mail does not enjoy the same legal protection from interception as do postal mail and telephone communications. As a general matter, for example, it is not illegal today to intercept another person's e-mail. The contents of an e-mail exchange are discoverable in legal proceedings; postal mail or telephone conversations typically are not. And prohibitions against mail or wire fraud do not yet clearly apply to e-mail communications. Many of the protections that now apply to other forms of communication will have to be extended to networked digital communications if the latter are to carry sensitive information.[14] Will the act of reading an official e-mail (such as a summons, a tax notice, or some other communication that requires the recipient to take action) be construed as proof that the message was received, much as a signature for certified postal mail is today? Could a subpoena be served by e-mail? And what responsibility will citizens have to check e-mail regularly for official documents?

Key escrow. There is current uncertainty and controversy about the laws and regulations that will govern the use of encryption for secure communication within the United States. Will users of so-called strong encryption be required to register their keys with "key escrow" facilities so that law enforcement agencies can decipher communications if necessary? If so, who will maintain these escrows? How and how well can these key depositories—arguably among the most

---

[14]The European Union is considerably more aggressive than the United States in mandating privacy protections in telecommunications (see Mayer-Schönberger, 1999).

attractive targets for the criminally inclined—be protected? Must escrow holders be independent of CAs or independent of government agencies to minimize chances for abuse? Under what circumstances can or should escrow holders be required to disclose keys to law enforcement personnel? Presumably, there should be no requirement for escrow of keys used purely for the purposes of establishing digital signatures, since such keys establish only identity and integrity of messages. But is it possible to guarantee that keys intended only for digital signature purposes cannot also be used for encryption?

Multiple laws and standards. In the past few years, a number of states have enacted digital signature legislation that endows electronic documents meeting specified standards with the same status as traditional signed paper documents. Unfortunately, requirements for a valid digital signature vary from state to state. Little progress has been made toward national standards for shared trust that will facilitate cross-jurisdictional transactions. International standards are yet further off. Neither has progress been made toward security standards that will be acceptable for multiple government transactions. It is quite unlikely, in fact, that a single security standard for many government interactions is practical or desirable. Should, for example, information about recent traffic violations be protected at the same level as tax returns or health information? Making all communications with government agencies meet the security standards of the most sensitive would doubtless increase the cost and inconvenience associated with many communications. One might envision a hierarchy of digital authority certificates being granted, much like the four levels of assurance (rudimentary, basic, medium, high) of the Bridge PKI hub system being developed under the auspices of the Federal Public Key Infrastructure Steering Committee.

Who will pay? Secure communication will not be costless. Who will bear these costs? Will citizens who wish to communicate with government agencies via the Internet be required to pay Internet access charges and CA subscription fees just as citizens who wish to communicate with a government agency today are required to pay for postage or telephone service? Will CA services be available on a subscription basis (like basic local telephone service), and will it be feasible or desirable to charge users for actual usage (like long-distance telephone service)? Can or should the government provide basic

CA services for any citizen willing to use a centralized government-managed service?

Relations among CAs. To what extent will multiple CAs have to co-operate? A degree of interoperability would seem desirable so that by checking with his or her own CA a user could conveniently confirm the validity of a correspondent's public key, even if that key had been issued by a different CA. This kind of interoperability will require that a "web of trust" develop among CAs and that all CAs in the web meet some minimum standards. By establishing standards for identities used for government transactions, government agencies might help to build this web of trust. But which agencies and which standards? And whose responsibility will it be to monitor CAs to guarantee that standards are being maintained? Is self-policing among CAs adequate for these purposes?

Other issues transcending security matters involve the possibility of providing universal e-mail addresses for all citizens and providing convenient access for all citizens to these services. These other issues related to the implementation of effective government-citizen communication are discussed below.

Tokens. Joan Q. Citizen wants to send a personalized message to the SSA, expects its content to remain private and untampered with, and both she and the agency want assurance that it is really from her, not someone "spoofing" her identity. As indicated above, such assurances can be obtained through the use of digital certificates, issued by CAs, that bind a digital public/private key pair to her identity and possibly to other key pairs to various authorizations she has been granted regarding access to data, ability to change her account information, and so on.

As mentioned earlier, such key pairs would likely be stored in one's PC—perhaps within a file acting as a digital wallet containing various such certificates—for access by computer and communication programs as needed.

There are, however, three main disadvantages to the above scheme. First, someone else accessing Joan's computer (and perhaps knowing her SSN, mother's maiden name, and a simple password she uses to protect the PC's digital wallet file) might easily forge her identity in various transactions. Second, if those digital certificates are stored on her home desktop PC, she might not be able to conduct transactions from another PC (e.g., while traveling or at work). Third, if the PC is often hooked to the Internet, it is possible for a snooping program to be inadvertently triggered or downloaded (e.g., during the use of a browser or e-mail program) to search for such files and surreptitiously retrieve them over the Internet for subsequent misuse.

The solution to all of the above problems is to embed Joan's digital certificates in a physical "token" of some sort, not unlike the plastic credit cards she carries in her wallet. Most likely, that token would be a credit-card-like smart card containing a small computer chip and memory, capable of interacting with a card reader attached to a PC to authenticate the holder of that card by transmitting on request the relevant digital certificate(s) stored within it. A simple password or PIN would probably be used to "unlock" the smart card so that someone stealing or finding the card would not have instant access to Joan's accounts and permissions.

The great majority of PCs today do not have smart card readers attached, but we expect many—especially in public access areas—to have such devices in the future, for reasons such as those illustrated in our example. Joan would therefore be able to conduct her personalized, secure transactions from a variety of workstations nationwide if not worldwide.

What, then, are the issues regarding such tokens? One is the burden placed on users, some of them elderly, uneducated, poor and/or infirm in various ways, to retain and access this token when needed. HCFA, for one, prides itself on not requiring any such identification card or other token from its constituents when they access Medicare facilities. Would such tokenization of electronic transactions break this tradition and therefore be unacceptable?

More generally, would the requirement of a smart card for various government services come too close to the notion of a national identification card, to which many object?

Another, perhaps lesser, issue is the bureaucracy needed to handle a token system: creating and sending tokens to authorized users, and quickly invalidating lost or stolen ones and then replacing them. (How do you know the request for a new card to replace a lost one is valid, given that the requester does not have the digital certificate validating his or her identity?) This is essentially the same problem handled routinely by today's credit-card companies. Perhaps a solution to both the "government ID" problem and the token-handling problem is that various private CAs, such as VeriSign, will issue "private-label" smart cards, so that the customer has a choice of providers and there is no one universally required source. In any such solution, the token should be viewed as a convenience, not a necessity.

Another possible solution to the token problem is biometrics: using physical attributes such as a fingerprint, retinal scan, or voice print to positively identify those conducting transactions with an agency. However, these are most relevant in protected, fixed installations. They are unlikely to become widespread on individuals' PCs, due both to expense and to the need for their operation to be tamper-proof and unspoofable.

GETTING FROM HERE TO THERE

Routine, secure e-mail communication between government agencies and individual citizens will not become a reality overnight. Considerable groundwork must be laid: Standards for confidentiality, integrity, nonrepudiation, and authentication must be established; CAs must be identified or established; a host of institutional, administrative, and policy questions have to be resolved; and, most important, accumulating experience and maturing laws, regulations, and practice norms will have to provide a foundation for trust in using e-mail for sensitive communications.

The task of creating a capability for secure communication between governments and citizens is a daunting one. How can we begin to put the necessary pieces in place?

An incremental, experimental approach is key. Experience with on-line transactions is steadily accumulating. Users are gradually becoming comfortable with the notion of entrusting sensitive information to the Internet. Government agencies are learning about public expectations for service and security and about the procedures necessary to provide both. With attitudes and capabilities changing so rapidly, it will be important not to lock into a single approach to secure communication. The temptation to let the ever better become the enemy of the adequate will be strong, but the likelihood that the system will be entirely right on the first try is vanishingly small, and there is little point in trying at the outset for a system that will meet all government demands. Much better to concentrate on functional requirements and to experiment, starting with relatively undemanding applications and relatively nonsensitive information, and then to gradually strengthen systems and procedures until there is confidence that the most complex transactions and the most sensitive data can be handled. In other words, how to renew dog licenses over the Internet should be figured out before income tax return filing is attempted.

Citizens should be able to "opt in." At least during a transition period, when the security and reliability of on-line communication with government agencies is still being demonstrated, citizens must be able to opt in to such communication arrangements, positively choosing for their records or accounts to be accessible on-line. Simply allowing citizens to opt out—i.e., to block electronic access to their personal information by themselves or anyone else—will probably be inadequate. It is premature to assume that citizens have sufficient understanding of the implications of on-line access and of procedures to control this access to make on-line access the default option.

"Out of band" communication will continue to be important. To provide adequate assurance of the identity of an individual, it is often useful to use a separate channel of communication for verification. For example, although application for a digital identity certificate might be made on-line or in person, the password or PIN unlocking or activating the certificate might be sent by postal mail to the correspondent's registered home address. Similarly, requests to establish specific authority may be transmitted and verified through separate channels or through channels different from those used to exercise the authority. Particularly sensitive transactions may require confirmation through independent channels. All of this suggests that policy should aim to maintain and to utilize multiple channels for electronic communication: the Internet, automated telephone services, bank ATM networks, and the like.

Success will depend on education and training. Successful development and deployment of mechanisms for digital communication between citizens and governments will require extensive efforts to educate citizens regarding the advantages of new communication modes and associated protections for sensitive information. Training in how to establish, use, and protect a digital identity will also be key. Equally important will be establishing realistic expectations among users. Just because e-mail can be transmitted nearly instantaneously, for example, users cannot expect instantaneous answers to queries. Current modes of postal and telephone communication—and all the procedures, customs, and expectations that go with them—have evolved over decades. The evolution of legal precedents, operational procedures, and social practices and norms relating to e-mail communication will also require time.

Chapter Six

CITIZENS, COMPUTERS, AND CONNECTIVITY:
A REVIEW OF TRENDS

As each new medium of communication has emerged, "its proponents have pointed out its value not only to the owners and early users, but to the broader society as well" (Firestone and Garner, 1998, pp. v–xi). In this respect, digital communication media do not differ from their predecessors. The Clinton/Gore administration, for example, announced expectations that the Internet would serve as a vehicle to "reinvent government" and "transform society" (National Partnership for Reinventing Government, 1993). And, according to a recent National Research Council report, computing and communication technologies and associated enterprises had advanced enough by the early 1990s "to be accepted as public infrastructure" (National Research Council, Computer Science and Telecommunications Board, 1997a, pp. 1–6).

Not surprisingly, the strategic plans of many government agencies assume the widespread availability of such an infrastructure. The Office of Management and Budget, for instance, expects that "75 percent of all transactions between individuals and the government— including such services as delivery of food stamps, Social Security benefits, and Medicaid information—will take place electronically" (The Benton Foundation, 1998, pp. 1–8). But are these aims realizable?

Our case studies of two agencies (see Chapters Three and Four) suggest that e-mail could be used to handle individualized communications between government services and their citizen clients in ways that would potentially yield both cost savings and quality improvements. Chapter Five reviews key technical and institutional barriers to making the national information infrastructure useful for the conduct of such official interactions. Here we examine trends in accessibility of computers and networked digital media to the government's clients.

At an aggregate level, the continuing rapid expansion of the electronic communication infrastructure is unquestionable (see Figure 6.1). A 1995 RAND report cited the number of Internet host machines in that year as over 6.7 million; by now, that number exceeds 30 million (Anderson et al., 1995). Internet traffic continues to grow at a dramatic rate as well, reportedly doubling every six to nine months (National Research Council, Computer Science and Telecommunications Board, 1997b, pp. 7–9). Further, among current Internet users who responded to a Forrester Research Inc. survey, the most common network activity by far is e-mail, reported by over 88 percent of households that had been on-line at least three times in the previous three months.[1]

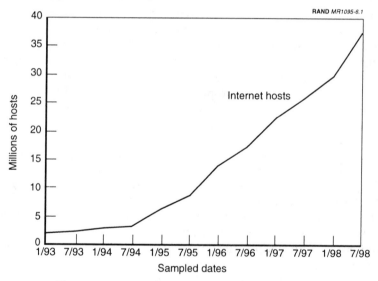

Figure 6.1—Growth in Internet Hosts, 1993–1998

---

[1]"Entertainment Technology," *Wall Street Journal*, March 22, 1999. This special section presents results of a survey of 100,000 North American households with both computers and network access.

While encouraging, such aggregate statistics do not provide a picture of how evenly computer and communication technologies are distributed over the country's varied demographic constituencies. "Looming large," for instance, "is the concern that the Internet may be accessible only to the most affluent and educated members of our society," according to a recent article in *Science* (Hoffman and Novak, 1998). Future policies for governmental and societal uses of these advanced media will be critically affected by the breadth and equity of their reach.

As we argued in our earlier report (Anderson et al., 1995), the societal advantages of a networked information and communication infrastructure cannot be fully realized until there is approximately universal service.[2] For this, it is important to provide an updated understanding of trends in citizen access to computers and networks in the United States.

REVIEWING CURRENT TRENDS

In this chapter, we present a detailed review of trends in access to computers and communication networks in the U.S. population. The review parallels and updates trends discussed in our earlier report (Anderson et al., 1995). Here, however, we include data from the October 1997 Current Population Survey (CPS), along with data gathered from similar surveys in October of 1993, 1989, and 1984 (U.S. Bureau of the Census, 1998, 1994, 1990, and 1985).

The CPS is a large-scale random-sample survey of households conducted monthly by the Bureau of the Census. It is the source for much of the official data published by the Bureau of Labor Statistics. The Bureau of the Census periodically adds supplements to the CPS base questionnaires to gain more insight into topics of interest. In this review, as in the earlier study, we chose supplements for examination that include comparable questions on computer use by each individual in a household. However, since the 1984 questions are not always comparable to those asked in later years, we rely chiefly on

---

[2]See also National Research Council, Computer Science and Telecommunications Board, 1997, pp. 29–31.

data from the more recent surveys, examining 1984 data only in relation to the availability of a personal computer in the household.[3]

Approach to the CPS Data

CPS data are suitable for analysis at the household or individual level. Our study treats the individual as the unit of analysis. Although some outcomes of interest (e.g., presence of a computer at home) are readily interpretable at either level, others (especially behavioral variables, such as use of networked services) are not. However, where both levels of analysis are appropriate, patterns of findings at the individual and household levels do not differ.

At the individual level, the statistical analyses we describe below are based in the main on 266,378 observations (123,249 in 1997 and 143,129 in 1993); some figures and tables also represent data from 1989 and 1984 (based on 146,850 and 151,832 observations, respectively). In every year, the sample comprises noninstitutionalized civilians in the United States living in households. Both adults and children are in the sample.[4] The analyses were done using individual weights that approximately equal the inverse of the probability of being in the sample, adjusted for interview response rates and normalized to add up to the sample size.

Outcome variables. To represent access to information and communication technology, we employ two binary outcome variables defined as they were in our earlier report (Anderson et al., 1995, pp. 20–21). One, access to a computer at home, is a single-item measure; it receives a positive value if there is a computer in an individual's household. At this level of analysis, penetration of computers refers to the percentage of individuals with household access (rather than the percentage of households that have computers). Strictly speaking, we measure presence of a computer in the household irrespective of ownership. We assume that all household members have access to a computer present in the household.

---

[3]Most notably, the 1984 CPS did not solicit information about use of e-mail or other network-based activity.

[4]Questions about computer and network use are asked only in reference to persons 3 years or older.

The other outcome variable, use of network services, represents use of a computer either at home or at work to connect to an electronic network. A derived measure, this variable receives a positive value if an individual uses a computer in any one of the following ways:

- At home to connect to bulletin boards;

- At home to connect to a computer at work;

- At work for communications (seen as distinct from word processing, desktop publishing, newsletter creation, and so on);

- At home or at work for e-mail.

It is important to include connectivity in the workplace as well as from home in the definition because it provides a more complete picture of the degree to which individuals use electronic avenues to communicate with others. In 1997, more individuals reported using network services at home (15 percent) than at work (13 percent); this contrasts with data obtained in 1993, when workplace users still outnumbered home users. However, as before, there is considerable overlap among them. For example, over 40 percent of those who access a network from their workplace also do so from home.[5] Overall trends for the two outcome variables are shown in Figure 6.2. The penetration of home computers increased from 18 percent in 1989 to 27 percent in 1993 and 42 percent in 1997. Moreover, by 1997 about a quarter of the people in computerized households had access to two or more computers there.[6] The use of network services from either home or work increased from 6 percent in 1989 to 11 percent in 1993 and 23 percent in 1997. Among those with a home computer, however, 42 percent reported use of network services in 1997.

---

[5]The CPS does not directly obtain information about the nature of network use for individualized communication from schools and libraries. It is important to note that access to the Web does not necessarily imply access to an e-mail account (and vice versa). If responses indicating school-based use (as reported by parents) are added to the derived variable representing network service use, the total number of network users increases by less than 1 percent (a statistically negligible amount), but an unhelpful ambiguity about the definition of network use is created. For these reasons, we did not include parents' reports of children's school-based use of a network in defining this outcome variable.

[6]In 1997, the CPS added a question asking how many computers there were if the initial question about the presence of a computer at home was answered positively.

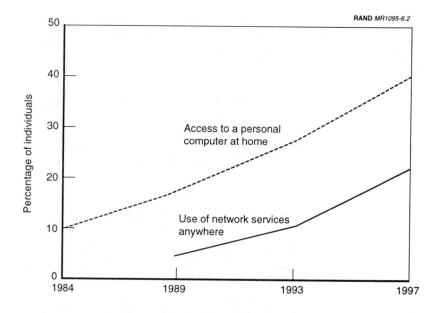

Figure 6.2—U.S. Census/CPS Data

Predictor variables. Six predictor variables constitute the core of our review of trends: income, education, race/ethnicity, age, sex, and location of residence.[7] Income, a categorical variable defined by quartiles, refers to the total income of the individual's household. Location, another variable defined at the household level, reflects whether the individual lives in an urban or a rural area. Remaining predictor variables refer only to the individual. Each explanatory variable is further described in our discussion of results, below.

Analysis plan. In investigating the CPS data, our goal was to learn whether and, if so, how socioeconomic characteristics are correlated with distribution patterns and diffusion trends in access to computers and digital networks. Figure 6.2 presents aggregated CPS data

---

[7]Our analyses are intended to be descriptive without taking a position on the direction of causality. It may be the case that the presence of a home computer makes someone more productive and thereby increases his or her income. We ignore such potential reverse causality and treat the socioeconomic characteristics as independent predictor variables.

representing the two outcome variables of interest for the U.S. population in 1997, 1993, and 1989 (and, for access to a computer at home, in 1984). The analysis was designed to answer two questions about these outcomes at the individual level:

- In 1997, in comparison to their proportion of the population, are any socioeconomically defined groups significantly underrepresented among those with computers at home and those who use network services anywhere?

- How have recent trends contributed to the present-day distribution of outcomes? That is, have differences between groups in access to computers and communication technology narrowed, remained constant, or widened over recent years?

Answers to these questions are tested statistically in several ways. First, we examined differences in access to a computer at home and use of network services across socioeconomic groups separately for each year for which data are available. These differences, generated by cross-tabulations, are shown in graphs of trends for each socioeconomic variable of interest. Because of very large sample sizes, comparisons between groups for all socioeconomic dimensions and for each year of study are generally statistically significant; when they are not, we explicitly note the absence of difference.[8]

For purposes of policy analysis and intervention, however, these "gross" differences may be misleading. Socioeconomic status variables are likely to be intercorrelated, meaning that an effort to investigate any one of them should control for the potential influence of the others.[9] Therefore, we also held constant the other predictor

---

[8]Statistical significance is determined here on the basis of the Pearson chi-square test. Note that all weights are normalized to add up to the sample size.

[9]For example, suppose it is a policy goal to provide equal use of network services across socioeconomic groups. As we show below, black individuals tend to use network services to a lesser extent than whites. This may prompt policymakers to direct efforts to increase use of network services to black communities. However, as we also show, low-income individuals likewise tend to make less use of network services than do high-income individuals. And because the average household income among blacks is lower than among whites, it may be the case that part or all of the racial/ethnic difference is due to income differentials. More-equal use of network services across socioeconomic groups, then, might be achieved more effectively by targeting poor communities generally rather than black communities specifically.

variables studied, in order to recalculate the cross-tabulations based on such "net" percentages. Net figures can be interpreted as representing differences between individuals in access to computers and use of networks based on one socioeconomic dimension only, with otherwise equal characteristics. The same general pattern of findings emerges from the net data as from the unadjusted data, but net differences generally tend to be smaller.

Finally, we were interested in whether the gaps between socioeconomic groups narrowed, stayed the same, or widened between 1993 and 1997. There are several ways to measure changes in penetration gaps. Consider the discrepancy in access to a home computer between individuals in the bottom and top income quartiles. As we show below, 7 percent of individuals in the bottom income quartile and 55 percent of those in the top income quartile had a home computer in 1993; by 1997, these penetration rates had grown to 15 and 75 percent, respectively. At the gross level, the income-based gap was 48 percentage points in 1993 and widened to 60 percentage points in 1997. However, adoption of new technologies tends to be fairly slow at low penetration levels, faster thereafter, and slower again as it reaches saturation, so it is not immediately obvious that the lower incomes fell farther behind. An alternative measure is, for example, the period of time it will take the bottom quartile to achieve the same penetration rate as the top quartile enjoyed at the time of the survey. That is, how long will it take the bottom quartile to grow from its 1993 level of 7 percent to the 55 percent of the top quartile, and how long will it take to increase penetration from its 1997 level of 15 percent to the top quartile's 75 percent? Has the penetration lag lengthened, stayed the same, or shortened between 1993 and 1997?

Appendix A explains in detail how we test for changes between 1993 and 1997 in such lags or gaps. We develop logit models of access to a home computer and use of network services based on pooled 1993 and 1997 data, and estimate the extent to which coefficients have changed between 1993 and 1997. The models are multivariate; that is, we test only for changes in "net" gaps (see Table A.1). The appendix also provides a table with both gross and net percentage data for the two outcome variables for 1989, 1993, and 1997 for purposes of comparison (see Table A.2).

The following discussion emphasizes gross results, but we systematically point out where and to what extent these results overstate disparities across socioeconomic groups.

Results of Data Analysis

In what follows, findings from the data analysis are presented separately for each of the six predictor variables.

Differences by household income. Figures 6.3 and 6.4 show, respectively, trend data representing the percentage of individuals reporting that there is a computer in the household and that they use network services, as a function of household income category. We distinguish four income categories, chosen such that each captures approximately 25 percent of the population. In 1997, the quartile cutoff income levels were $20,000, $35,000, and $60,000 per year.[10]

As is immediately clear in Figure 6.3, there are very large differences in household computer ownership across income categories. In 1997, about 15 percent of the lowest-income households had computers at home, whereas about 75 percent of the highest-earning quartile did. Four years earlier, the respective figures were around 7 percent and 55 percent. These data, then, continue to reflect highly significant differences in household computer access based on income.

The net disparities, controlling for the other key socioeconomic variables we studied, are not quite as large, but they remain substantial. For example, in 1997, on net, individuals in the top income quartile were over three times more likely than those in the bottom quartile to have access to a computer in the household (see Appendix A, Table A.2). This net income-based gap is smaller than the gross figure, mostly because low-income individuals tend to have lower than average educational attainment. Specifically, about a third of

---

[10]Income quartile is based on total family income, i.e., the combined income of all family members aged 15+ during the past 12 months. (Households that did not provide an income figure are missing from our tabulations by income.) The CPS does not contain exact dollar figures; income is reported in 14 categories. We further collapsed those categories into four such that each contains roughly 25 percent of the respondents: Q1 (the bottom quartile) represents 26.1 percent; Q2, 22.5 percent; Q3, 26.3 percent; and Q4, 25.1 percent (all weighted).

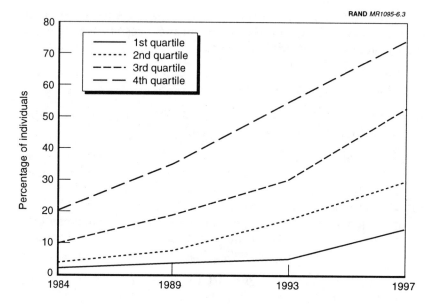

Figure 6.3—People in Computer Households, by Income

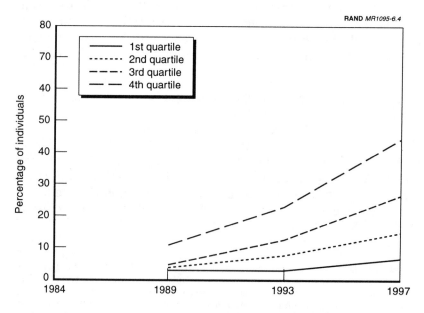

Figure 6.4—People Using Network Services, by Income

the income disparity is attributable to a concomitant effect from educational differences. These data thus continue to reflect highly significant differences in home computer access based on income.

Further, while the income-based gap in computer ownership was wide in 1993, it was even wider by 1997. Evidence for this finding comes from inspecting differences in percentages between the top and bottom quartiles in the two years: in 1993 these households differed by about 48 percent with respect to computer ownership; in 1997, the difference between these quartiles was about 60 percentage points. As explained above, such gross level gaps do not necessarily indicate that the bottom income quartile has fallen further behind. Our multivariate analysis of the change in the net discrepancy, however, indicates that the income-based gap did indeed widen somewhat between 1993 and 1997 (see Appendix A, Tables A.1 and A.2).

Although the extent of network service use either at home or at work is far less than the extent of household computer availability (see Figure 6.4), generally similar patterns appear for network use as a function of household income level.[11] Again, we find large differences between quartiles that tend to persist over time. In 1993, close to 3 percent of the lowest-income individuals used network services at home or work, whereas 23 percent of the highest income individuals used them. By 1997, these fractions had increased to 7 percent and about 45 percent, respectively. As before, conducting these same tests using net rather than gross figures yields somewhat smaller but still highly significant income-based differences in network service use.

Moreover, whether gross or net figures are used, differences in use of network services between the highest and lowest income groups have continued unabated. The trend lines, for example, show about a 20 percent difference in extent of network access between the top and bottom quartiles in 1993; by 1997, the gap between them has nearly doubled, to 38 percent (see also Appendix A, Table A.2, to

---

[11]Recall that our measure of network use includes use at home or work but not at school, since the appropriate questions were not asked directly of students. This implies that we are likely to overstate differences in network use across income categories, because students who live away from their parents tend to have low household incomes.

compare net percentages). Statistical tests based on the prediction model plus assessments of how income and time interact with this outcome show that this gap in network use between individuals in the top and bottom income quartiles remained constant between 1993 and 1997 when other influences are controlled (see Appendix A, Table A.1). The size of the gap between the bottom quartile and the third quartile also remained unchanged during those years while the gap between the second quartile and the bottom quartile decreased.

We thus conclude that there are large differences in both household computer ownership and use of network services across income categories. These differences are partly due to other socioeconomic characteristics, but they remain substantial even after controlling for those other characteristics. To help concretize these differences, Appendix A presents a stylized penetration model (see Figure A.1). If the penetration rates for home computers keep increasing at the 1993–1997 pace, for example, then an individual in the bottom income quartile in 1997 could be expected to lag those in the top quartile by about nine years in obtaining access to a computer at home. If these same assumptions are applied to use of network services, the time lag for adoption of these new media between the bottom quartile and the top, other things being equal, is just over two years (see Appendix A).

These results appear to be consistent with conclusions about income-based differences in access to computers and network service use reported in other recent studies (Katz and Aspden, 1996; Hoffman, Novak, and Venkatesh, 1998; National Telecommunications and Information Administration, 1998). Moreover, they provide partial support for the view that lack of a computer at home is a major barrier to network access among low-income groups. First, home computer gaps are larger than and growing more steadily than gaps in network access. Second, gaps in the use of network services are smaller in part because of access provided in the workplace, where individual employees do not have to pay for hardware and connectivity. However, it is usually employees in relatively higher level and better paid positions whose jobs are associated with e-mail use (Kreuger, 1993). Finally, there is clear agreement about there being considerable "churn" among Internet users, although estimated rates vary.[12] In any case, according to the national survey done by Katz and Aspden, "the key reported reason [why former users stopped using the Internet] was loss of access to a computer" (Katz and Aspden, 1996). It appears, then, that rapidly improving price/performance ratios for computers in recent years have not served to narrow (or even to hold constant) the digital divide.

Differences by educational attainment. Figures 6.5 and 6.6 show data for differences by educational attainment. Figure 6.5 presents household computer availability fractions for individuals without a high school diploma, for high school graduates, and for college graduates. (For purposes of this analysis, those still enrolled in primary school, secondary school, or undergraduate college were excluded from the dataset.) Persons with some college education, but without a bachelor's degree and not currently enrolled in a school, are included among high school graduates. As might be expected, there are large differences in household computer access by educational attainment.

Among persons without a high school diploma, only about 9 percent had a home computer in 1993. College graduates, by contrast, had a penetration rate of about 49 percent. All groups experienced an increase in home computers between 1993 and 1997, leading to penetration rates of about 17 percent and 66 percent in 1997 for those without a high school diploma and for college graduates, respectively. Controlling for other socioeconomic characteristics, the differences are substantially smaller but still highly significant statistically in both years (see net percentages in Appendix A, Table A.2).

In the intervening four years, these education-based differences in access to household computers have held steady. That is, although the gross percentage gap has widened between the upper and lower education levels, the increase, on net, is not statistically significant.

---

[12]The churn rate refers to the proportion of people who once used the Internet but have stopped using it, compared to the total number who have ever used it. Katz and Aspden (1996) estimate the churn rate at 50 percent, while Hoffman, Novak, and Venkatesh (1998) estimate it at 20 to 30 percent. The difference in estimates is a function of the length of the nonuse period set as the criterion for defining dropouts. Regardless of the criterion selected, the churn rate is substantial and warrants further investigation.

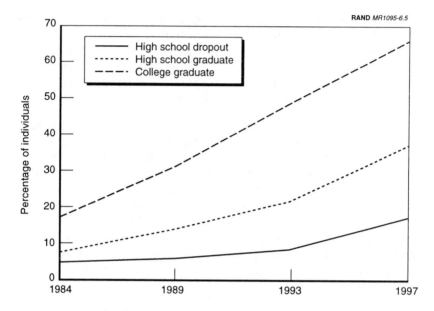

Figure 6.5—People in Computer Households, by Education

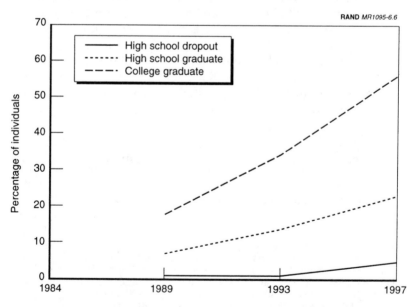

Figure 6.6—People Using Network Services, by Education

These findings result both from the prediction equation we tested and from testing the significance of the interaction between year and education level as an influence on likelihood of having a home computer (see Appendix A, Table A.1). Thus, the patterns of education-related differences are rather similar to but less sharp than the income-based differences in household computer access reported above.

Figure 6.6 shows the differences in network service use by education category. Not surprisingly, perhaps, we find that use of network services is strongly dominated by well-educated individuals. In 1993, just over 1 percent of individuals without high school diplomas used network services, compared to about 34 percent of college graduates. Both groups greatly increased their network use in 1997, to just over 5 percent and about 56 percent, respectively. As expected, the net differences are smaller than these but nonetheless significant (see Appendix A, Table A.2).

Turning to the prediction equation, we learned that education-based gaps in use of network services between high school graduates and college graduates widened significantly from 1993 to 1997. This trend parallels the finding above related to income-based patterns of network use, where persistent or growing gaps are largely attributable to gains in access rates for the highest earning groups in those four years. It also parallels findings for education-based trends described in our 1995 report (Anderson et al., 1995), when increases in the network usage gap between 1989 and 1993 were largely explained by access growth for the most-educated group. By contrast, the size of the network access gap between high school dropouts and high school graduates actually narrowed between 1993 and 1997 (as did the network access gap between the bottom two income quartiles).

In summary, we find large differences in access to information and communication technology by educational attainment that are, with the notable exception of the narrowed gap in network use between high school dropouts and high school graduates, either holding steady or widening over time. Again, these results are consistent with findings from other national sample studies (Katz and Aspden, 1996; Hoffman, Kalsbeek, and Novak, 1996). Further, these education-based differences persist after accounting for income differences. Given the correlation between use of network services and knowledge of current political, professional, and organizational affairs described in the earlier report, these results suggest that disparities in access to network technologies may work to amplify differential knowledge produced by differing education levels alone.

Such differences are additionally problematic because of their potential influence on children's educational opportunities. If there is a computer at home, about 72 percent of those age 19 and younger will use it (see Appendix A, Table A.3). Further, our review of the CPS children's questionnaire data indicates that, among students age 14 and younger, over 47 percent use the home computer specifically for educational programs (46.9 percent of boys and 49.5 percent of girls). These findings are consistent with other research showing few differences in patterns of children's computer use if access gaps based on parental income and education are overcome (Kraut et al., 1996).

Differences by race and ethnicity. Recent studies have raised concerns that African Americans and Hispanics are lagging behind in the use of digital media (Hoffman and Novak, 1998; Wilhelm, 1998). At least part of the race- and ethnicity-based difference is due to lower average household income and lower average educational attainment among these groups, as compared to non-Hispanic whites. However, our analysis shows that these characteristics do not account for the entire difference in outcome variables. Rather, racial and ethnic characteristics exert an independent and important influence on home computer access and network use.

For purposes of our analysis, we combine race and ethnicity to create a single variable with mutually exclusive categories. A five-level variable, it distinguishes Hispanics, non-Hispanic whites, non-Hispanic blacks, Native Americans (both Indians and Eskimos), and Americans of Asian descent (including Pacific Islanders). In subsequent comments, we refer to non-Hispanic whites as "whites" and to non-Hispanic blacks as "blacks." A small fraction of respondents are identified as "other" in the CPS data. We do not reflect the "other" category in the figures below (or in Table A.2 of Appendix A); however, predictive models and tests based on those models take into account the influence of that category along with the defined race/ethnicity groups. Figures 6.7 and 6.8 portray the percentage of

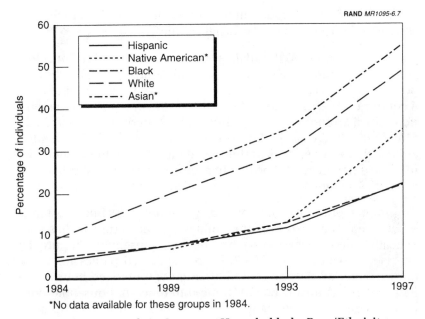

*No data available for these groups in 1984.

Figure 6.7—People in Computer Households, by Race/Ethnicity

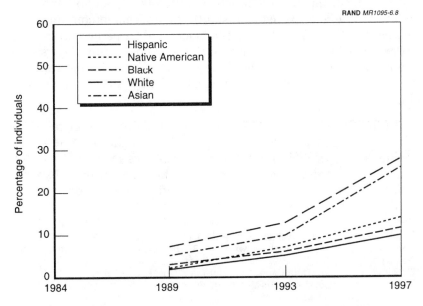

Figure 6.8—People Using Network Services, by Race/Ethnicity

individuals with a computer in the household and access to network services at home or at work by racial/ethnic categories.

As Figure 6.7 reveals, the highest penetration rates for household computers are found among whites and Asians. In 1997, about 49 percent of whites and 56 percent of Asians lived in a household with a computer. Hispanics and blacks, by contrast, reported a penetration rate of around 22 percent, and Native Americans, 35 percent. A remarkable increase in home computer penetration is evident among Native Americans in the 1997 data.[13] As we mentioned, part of these differences may be due to average differences in other characteristics, notably household income and educational attainment.

Controlling for these characteristics, we nonetheless find substantial differences. That is, net of other influences, race/ethnicity has a statistically independent and sizable effect on household computer access (see Appendix A, Table A.2). In particular, Hispanics and blacks are currently underrepresented among computerized households. Patterns of significant racial/ethnic difference in household computer access are also evident in the 1993 data. Since 1993, however, there have been some noteworthy changes in their relative size. Specifically, from 1993 to 1997 (when the influence of other socioeconomic variables is held constant), the household computer gap has widened significantly between blacks and Hispanics, on the one hand, and whites, on the other; has narrowed by a statistically significant margin between Native Americans and whites; and remains unchanged between Asian Americans and whites (see Appendix A, Table A.1).

It should, however, be underscored that the discrepancy between racial and ethnic groups is fairly small at the higher income levels. Home computer penetration among Hispanics in the top income quartile is 75 percent, not much below the rates for non-Hispanic whites (83 percent) and Asians (87 percent). Penetration rates for

---

[13]Native Americans are oversampled in the CPS. In 1993, 1,703 Native Americans were interviewed; in 1997, there were 1,763. By contrast, the Nielsen Internet Demographic Study (IDS) bases its 1996–1997 results on a sample that includes only 75 Native American respondents. See Hoffman, Novak, and Venkatesh, 1998, for a discussion of this and other issues involved in using Nielsen IDS data to make inferences about racial and ethnic differences in technology use.

blacks and Native Americans in the top income quartile are 66 and 79 percent, respectively.

Differential use of network services as a function of race/ethnicity is apparent in Figure 6.8. Again there are significant between-group differences, even when the influence of other socioeconomic characteristics is controlled. Net differences are also somewhat smaller than those observed for household computer access (see Appendix A, Table A.3), as expected. An examination of changes in gaps between 1993 and 1997, however, shows some surprising results.

In 1993, for instance, Asian Americans had the lowest net rate of network service use even though they had the highest net rate of household computer ownership among the racial/ethnic groups we studied. By 1997, the gap in network service use rates between this group and the highest penetration group (whites) had narrowed significantly, controlling for the influence of other socioeconomic variables; and it can be expected to close in the near future. In marked contrast, the gaps in network service use between blacks and Hispanics vs. socioeconomically similar whites widened significantly between 1993 and 1997, after having remained stable during the previous four years. For Native Americans, despite their substantial net gain in access to computers at home, the gap between them and socioeconomically similar whites in network service use remained constant from 1993 to 1997.

On the whole, then, we find rather large and persistent differences across race/ethnicity in both the availability of a household computer and the use of network services when the influence of other socioeconomic variables is controlled. These findings are consistent with results from other research on ethnic and racial gaps in access to digital media (National Telecommunications and Information Administration, 1998; Hoffman, Novak, and Venkatesh, 1998; Kraut et al., 1996). For instance, Hoffman and her colleagues point out that Asian Americans and Native Americans are—in net terms—among the most "wired" demographic groups, while African Americans and Hispanics are the least connected. The HomeNet study carried out by Kraut and his colleagues likewise finds race/ethnicity differences in technology use not explained by variation in income or education.

As we pointed out in our earlier report, we had not expected to find race/ethnicity differences in computer access and connectivity that were not attributable to variation in income, education, or other demographic characteristics. The size and endurance of the differences, however, indicate that race/ethnicity gaps deserve further investigation.

Differences by age. We now turn to differences by age.[14] In the figures that follow, for individuals between the ages of 20 and 60, we break down information about household computer access and network service use by decade. For analytic purposes, however, we rely on four categories, distinguishing between individuals under 20 years of age, between 20 and 39, between 40 and 59, and 60 years of age and older (preserving comparability with our earlier study). Boundaries based on age are admittedly arbitrary, and different studies employ different cutoffs and/or different numbers of categories. Particular boundary choices do not, however, appear to influence analytic results in ways that would affect most policy decisions.[15]

Figures 6.9 and 6.10 show age-related data on computer access and connectivity. As Figure 6.9 suggests, availability of a home computer is not marked by wide divisions between age-defined categories until about age 60, when rates of access to a household computer decline steeply. In 1997, around 40 to 50 percent of all individuals under age 60 had access to a home computer, whereas only about 20 percent of individuals above age 60 lived in a household with a computer. Even when other socioeconomic variables are controlled, this difference is

---

[14]The treatment of age is determined by the objectives of the study. The decision to purchase a computer is in part influenced by the size and composition of a household. However, our aim is to document socioeconomic and demographic differences in access to information and communication technology, rather than differences in personal ownership or use. The connection between presence of a computer at home and access to it requires only the relatively plausible assumption that the computer is available to all household members.

[15]In our exploratory analyses, we distinguished as many as eight different age categories. In Figures 6.9 and 6.10, we have retained six categories to permit inspection of outcome trends for individuals who are going to reach Medicare-eligible age levels in the relatively near term (see Chapter Three). However, for analysis purposes, we collapsed them into the four categories presented here and employed in our previous study, because the patterns that emerged were robust to this more parsimonious classification.

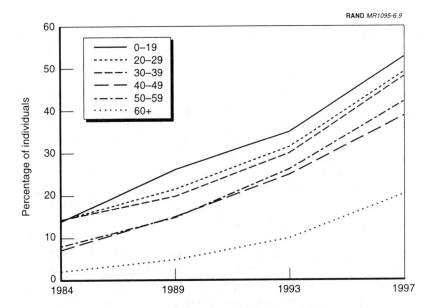

Figure 6.9—People in Computer Households, by Age

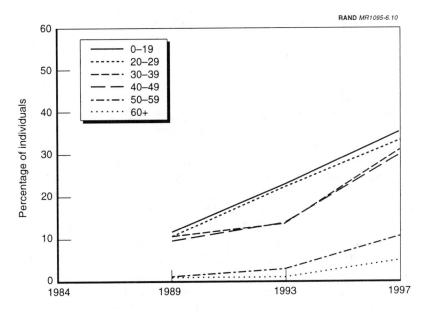

Figure 6.10—People Using Network Services, by Age

highly significant (see Appendix A, Table A.1). Moreover, while age-based gaps have remained essentially constant across the other age groups since 1993, the gap in home computer ownership for the over-60 group has increased significantly (Appendix A, Table A.2).

Figure 6.10 additionally reveals the existence of large differences in the use of network services across the age categories defined. Gross percentages suggest disparities at both ends of the age range, even though the youngest group overtook the oldest. In 1997, about 7 percent of all individuals age 60 and older, and about 11 percent of all individuals under age 20, reportedly used network services; these figures compare with over 33 percent of all people between the ages of 20 and 59 who used network services. However, these figures are quite different from net percentages that control for other socioeconomic variables (see Appendix A, Table A.2). When other characteristics are controlled, the gap between younger individuals and those age 20 to 59 in use of network services is substantially decreased. Older adults, in contrast, make markedly less use of network services than any other age group, and the difference remains large and significant even after the influence of other socioeconomic variables is controlled. Further, the gaps in network use between all individuals over age 40 and their demographically similar counterparts in the younger adult age group (20 to 39) has increased substantially from 1993 to 1997.

As we noted earlier, it is possible that the measure of network use employed here underrepresents students' access to on-line services, because no CPS questions directly addressed network use at school. However, recent careful studies of wired schools indicate that even where computers and connectivity are available, there is very little network service use on the part of students at school (Schofield, 1995; Schofield and Davidson, 1997). Moreover, these technologies tend to be largely available in schools attended by students from higher-income households who also have access at home. A recent Educational Testing Service (ETS) study concluded that minority and poor students had significantly less access to computers in their classes than did more-affluent children. Further, schools with a predominantly minority enrollment had an average student-computer ratio of 17 to 1, compared with the national average of 10 to 1; for computers with advanced graphics or interactive video, the discrepancies were even larger (Educational Testing Service, 1997).

These conclusions are corroborated, in part, by the detailed comparative study of Internet and Web use among black and white students carried out by Hoffman, Novak, and Venkatesh (1998). Their research found very large gaps in use of those technologies as a function of ethnicity; the difference was attributable to black students' relative lack of access to the Internet and Web outside of school, and especially to the lack of a home computer. A Yankelovich Monitor study similarly concludes that "what bars entry to cyberspace among African Americans" is not owning a home PC.[16]

We believe, then, that there have been substantial gains in connectivity for those at the lower end of the age range, but that the wiring of K–12 schools is probably not implicated in this trend. Rather, increased computer and network access at home probably accounts for this major change. In contrast, optimistic expectations for near-term connectivity gains among those over 60 (see Anderson et al., 1995) are disconfirmed by analyses of the 1997 data.

Differences by sex. Unlike our analyses based on the preceding socioeconomic variables, our analyses based on sex find little variation in access to home computers and use of network services, as Figures 6.11 and 6.12 illustrate. While the gross data shown in Figure 6.11 suggest a 2.5 percent discrepancy in rate of access to a computer at home in 1997, that gender difference disappears entirely when the influence of other socioeconomic variables is controlled (see Appendix A, net percentages in Table A.2,). Our previous report documented the closing of the real gender gap in household computer access between 1989 and 1993; 1997 data indicate that, even though availability of computers at home increased by more than 50 percent from 1993 to 1997, this equal access trend remained unchanged. It should be acknowledged, however, that data related to this outcome variable—having a computer at home—do not take into account which household member instigated the purchase of the computer or makes greatest use of it. For example, usage data presented in Appendix A (see Table A.3) show that men use a home computer much

---

[16]"More African Americans Plan to Go Online," *Interactive Daily,* February 18, 1997.

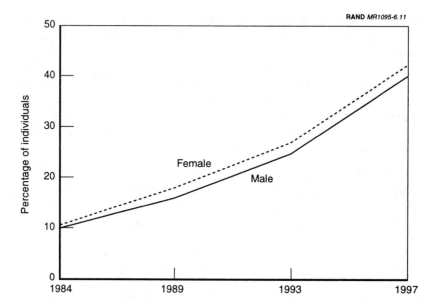

Figure 6.11—People in Computer Households, by Gender

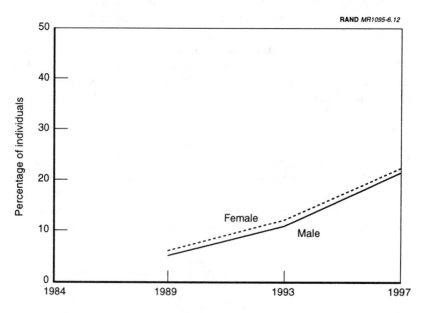

Figure 6.12—People Using Network Services, by Gender

more frequently than women do, even though they are approximately equally likely to be users if they have household access.

Figure 6.12 shows that use of network services exhibits similar variation as a function of sex when gross data are examined—a discrepancy of about 2.4 percentage points favoring male network users. When the influence of other socioeconomic variables is controlled, the size of the difference is much reduced but remains statistically significant (see Appendix A, Table A.2). This latter result is surprising, because analyses of data for both 1989 and 1993 produced no statistically significant gender differences in network use when the influence of other socioeconomic variables was held constant.

That this difference in network access has persisted and widened somewhat rather than disappeared over the most recent years for which CPS data are available conflicts with the general perception, expressed in our previous report as well as other studies, that the gender gap is closing (Hoffman, Novak, and Venkatesh, 1998; Sproull, in press). Although the net growth in the access gap during this period is fairly small (from a tenth of a percent difference in 1993 to 1 percent in 1997) and may have no social policy significance, CPS data provide a more reliable representation of the U.S. population than other data sources do. We therefore recommend continued careful tracking of gender-based trends in use of digital technologies in the next CPS supplements.

Differences by location of residence. Home computer penetration and access to network services as a function of residential location, the last predictor variable we explored in detail, are shown in Figures 6.13 and 6.14. Location is categorized as rural or urban, where "urban" characterizes residences within standard metropolitan areas as the census defines them.[17]

Ostensibly, the household computer penetration rate in urban areas is much higher than in rural areas. In 1997, about 45 percent of individuals living in an urban area had a computer at home, compared with about 35 percent among rural residents (see Figure 6.13). About

---

[17]These areas are defined using the Office of Management and Budget's June 30, 1984, definitions.

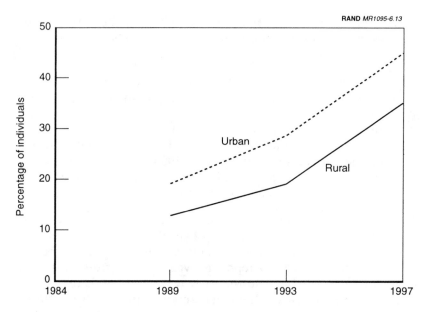

Figure 6.13—People in Computer Households, by Location

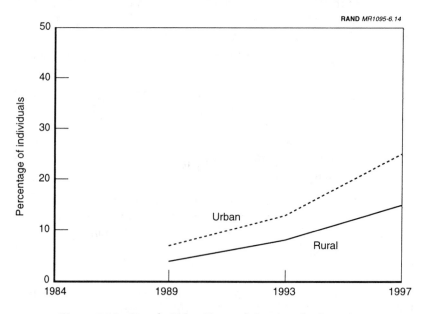

Figure 6.14—People Using Network Services, by Location

half of the difference is due to correlation with other characteristics, such as household income or education; nonetheless, the net gap is statistically significant. As pointed out in our earlier report, the urban-rural gap in home computer access had remained approximately constant between 1989 and 1993. Between 1993 and 1997, however, it narrowed significantly (see Appendix A, Tables A.1 and A.2).

There are also substantial gross differences in people's use of network services as a function of household location. About 25 percent of residents in urban areas made use of network services in 1997, whereas the figure is 15 percent for rural residents. Again, approximately half of the difference is due to characteristics such as income and education. However, when the influence of these characteristics is held constant, the gap remains. Further, the gap between rural and urban use of network services widened significantly between 1993 and 1997 (see Appendix A, Tables A.1 and A.2).

These analyses do not adequately reflect large-scale geographic variation in computers and connectivity. People living in the southeastern states, for instance, continue to lag people in all other regions in access to a computer at home (34 percent penetration rate) or to network services anywhere (18 percent penetration rate). Nor do our analyses do justice to the range of variation in digital media access to be found within particular urban or rural contexts. For instance, a study of distressed urban areas found that telephone and cable companies all too often have moved quickly to wire wealthier suburbs, bypassing poorer neighborhoods in the inner city. The lack of adequate telecommunications facilities makes problems not just for individuals but also for businesses, feeding a downward spiral in which lack of investment at the community level leads to fewer economic opportunities for the people who live there (Krieg, 1995). At the same time, unemployment, poverty, and outmigration have exacerbated the structural problems of many rural areas, according to one Office of Technology Assessment report. Today's high-technology businesses are attracted by a highly skilled work force plus network connections to other economic markets, which are what many rural areas lack (Office of Technology Assessment, 1991). Such more finely grained assessments provide an important complement to the large-scale analyses reported here.

CONCLUSIONS

Research carried out at RAND and elsewhere provides evidence that access to computers and communication networks influences opportunities to participate effectively in a range of economic, educational, social, and civic activities. The ability to interact with government agencies will soon be influenced by such technologies as well.

For these kinds of reasons, it is important to find out whether parts of the U.S. population are cut off from the emerging information society on the basis of their socioeconomic status. To address this question, our analyses sought to learn whether significant differences in access to these digital media existed in 1993 and 1997 and, if so, what had happened to the sizes of these differences over time. Table 6.1 serves as a score card summarizing the results we have discussed in this chapter.

While the score card does not present findings in numeric form, it highlights the main conclusions from detailed quantitative analyses: There is a "digital divide" between those who do and do not have access to computers and communication technologies; the division is significantly predicted by income, education, race/ethnicity, and—to a lesser extent—age, location, and possibly gender. For the most part, as Table 6.1 shows, these disparities have persisted over a period in which the technologies of interest have decreased dramatically in price (relative to what they can do) and increased markedly in user friendliness. More worrisome still, many of these socioeconomically based gaps have widened over this period.

These conclusions, drawn from a national sample of the U.S. population, are disturbing: Sizable demographic subgroups that remain on the wrong side of the digital divide may be deprived of the benefits associated with citizenship in an information society. In democracies, however, it is usually regarded as unfair to exclude individuals from the means for accessing information, communicating ideas, and participating in voluntary associations, civic organizations, and political activities (Anderson et al., 1995; Hochschild, 1981).

Further, as we pointed out in the introduction to this chapter, society as a whole loses out when broad and equitable access to these media

Table 6.1

Summary of Socioeconomic Findings

	Computer at Home			Use of Network Services		
	1997	1993	What Happened over Time to Gaps	1997	1993	What Happened over Time to Gaps
Income quartile						
Bottom vs. top	Yes	Yes	Widened	Yes	Yes	Constant
Bottom vs. 3rd	Yes	Yes	Widened	Yes	Yes	Constant
Bottom vs. 2nd	Yes	Yes	Constant	Yes	Yes	Narrowed
Education level						
High school vs. college	Yes	Yes	Constant	Yes	Yes	Widened
High school vs. dropout	Yes	Yes	Constant	Yes	Yes	Narrowed
Race/ethnicity						
White vs. Hispanic	Yes	Yes	Widened	Yes	Yes	Widened
White vs. black	Yes	Yes	Widened	Yes	Yes	Widened
White vs. Asian	Yes	Yes	Constant	Yes	Yes	Narrowed
White vs. Native Amer.	Yes	Yes	Narrowed	Yes	Yes	Constant
Age group						
20–39 vs. 60+	Yes	Yes	Widened	Yes	Yes	Widened
20–39 vs. 40–59	No	No	—	Yes	No	Widened
20–39 vs. 0–19	Yes	Yes	Widened	Yes	Yes	Narrowed
Sex: male vs. female	No	No		Yes	No	Widened
Location: urban vs. rural	Yes	Yes	Narrowed	Yes	Yes	Widened

is lacking. Thus, according to a recent NRC report (National Research Council, Computer Science and Telecommunications Board, 1997b, p. 30):

> As increasing fractions of the population become connected to a network, those left unconnected become an increasing burden on the democratic principle, and the cost of subsidizing their inclusion becomes smaller and smaller. Sooner or later the political calculus tips the balance toward a policy of guaranteeing universal service.

Our study of e-mail communications between government agencies and their citizen clients gives reasons for thinking that the shift should come soon, if governments are to realize the advantages of efficiency and quality potentially afforded by digital media. In 1982, *Time* magazine announced the arrival of the long-envisioned "information revolution" by naming the personal computer "Machine of the Year" (Sproull, in press). Now, over a decade and a half later, we still have only half a revolution (see Chapter One).

Chapter Seven

CONCLUSIONS, OBSERVATIONS, AND RECOMMENDATIONS

THE CASE FOR E-MAIL

A strong *prima facie* case can be made that government agencies whose work generates significant volumes of individualized communication should begin today to develop the means to use e-mail for this communication as a supplement to the more traditional, postal and telephonic channels. The principal elements of this argument are that

- **E-mail can be cheaper than postal or telephone communication,** for both government agencies and citizens. E-mail can effectively eliminate costs for stationery, printing, and postage. Well-structured digital documents can be filed, copied, routed, searched, transcribed, abstracted, checked for completeness and accuracy, and otherwise processed more efficiently and with less effort than can their paper or telephonic counterparts. In some applications, e-mail can be processed automatically and without direct human intervention, reducing agency staff time spent on low-level clerical tasks, smoothing fluctuations and staff workloads, and perhaps even allowing reductions in management and facility costs. Establishing a capability to communicate via e-mail will, of course, require substantial initial investments on the part of both agencies and individual citizens. Typically, maintaining e-mail service also requires regular payments to an Internet service provider (ISP). The evidence from our two case studies suggests that e-mail can bring substantial reductions in agency operating costs. The growing use of Internet and Web transactions by private-sector firms (airlines and brokerages are perhaps today's most prominent examples) provides further support for this proposition. Although detailed cost modeling was beyond the scope of this research, it seems likely that the reduced operating costs associated with large-volume applications of e-mail will more than offset the initial costs of creating governmental e-mail capabilities.

- **E-mail can allow improved service.** The speed with which e-mail is transmitted can reduce the time required to move information between citizens and governments. The asynchronous nature of e-mail communications can effectively extend government office hours, allowing citizens access when they find it convenient. If e-mail can be processed without direct human intervention, interactions can proceed in something close to real-time, and government offices can effectively provide round-the-clock service. If e-mail can be checked automatically for completeness and accuracy, some problems can be avoided or quickly straightened out. If agencies can agree on common user interfaces, e-mail can allow citizens "one-stop" access to a variety of government services. The use of a common e-mail "window" may save citizens from providing and government agencies from collecting the same information (name, date of birth, Social Security number [SSN], etc.) over and over again. Finally, e-mail can be sent from or received at many different locations, effectively "following" a mobile population.

- **Increased government use of e-mail may spur access to the Internet.** Many observers have commented on the potential social benefits that may result from increased access to the Internet and to e-mail. The value of one person's access to the Internet grows as more people have similar access. It is probably unrealistic to expect that making government services available on-line will encourage many more people to establish e-mail connections. Individual behavior is much more likely to be driven by the attractiveness of on-line entertainment, shopping, sports scores, and stock quotes than by anything that government agencies will make available. Nonetheless, as governments make more services available on-line, thinking about and support for increased public access to the Internet may increase. If nothing else, the very agencies that offer on-line services in the hopes of reducing operating costs will likely be forced to make increasing provision for the "unwired." Thus, efforts by government agencies to capture the efficiencies offered by e-mail may indirectly lead to improved access to e-mail.

- **Citizens will eventually insist on communicating with government agencies by e-mail.** It is already routine for many U.S. citizens to shop, execute financial transactions, make travel reservations, submit school assignments, and correspond with their relatives via the Internet and the World Wide Web. Increasingly and justifiably, they will expect similar ease in filing government documents, accessing government records, and transacting business with government agencies. Whatever the ultimate costs and benefits of e-mail communication, most government agencies will eventually have to support some sort of e-mail communication channel, because citizens will demand it. Developing these communication channels will not necessarily be straightforward, and it will behoove government agencies to begin planning for and experimenting with e-mail communication now.

Some nontrivial implementation and operation issues must be resolved before government agencies will be able to exploit e-mail fully. (We discuss these below.) Nonetheless, the case for increased use of e-mail by government agencies seems strong.

Our case studies of the federal Health Care Financing Administration (HCFA) and the California Employment Development Department (EDD) underline these potential advantages. The activities of each agency generate very large volumes of individualized communications that plausibly could be carried out by e-mail, resulting in lower costs and improved service. Interestingly, the most promising e-mail application for HCFA involves *sending* processed information—Medicare Summary Notices (MSNs)—to citizens. The most promising application for EDD appears to be *receiving* processible information—initial and continued claims for Unemployment Insurance (UI) benefits—from citizens.

SOME OPERATIONAL CONCERNS

Our case studies also identified a number of operational concerns associated with handling increasing volumes of e-mail communications with citizens. These concerns suggest that certain e-mail applications are more likely than others to succeed. They also point to some important preconditions for successful exploitation of e-mail.

Cost

Although e-mail offers an opportunity to make communication between government agencies and citizens cheaper and easier, both groups may have to bear some one-time costs in order to realize these benefits. Arguably, the costs of establishing basic connections to the Internet have either already been made by most government agencies and by many citizens or likely will be made independent of whether government agencies seek to expand their use of e-mail in communicating with individual citizens. Most government agencies, for example, already have e-mail systems that allow their staff to send internal messages and to access the Internet. Moreover, citizens who already own or have access to a computer and have established e-mail accounts to communicate with friends or business associates will face almost no additional costs if they decide to use their access to the Internet to communicate with government agencies. To the extent that these basic capabilities already or soon will exist for other reasons, the cost of creating them should not enter into the cost-benefit calculations of agencies considering increased use of e-mail.

But increased citizen-government interaction will require substantial investments beyond those for basic Internet connectivity. Agencies may have to acquire additional hardware to handle a much increased volume of e-mail transactions. Software to support specific e-mail applications will have to be written and tested. Web forms will have to be designed. Policies as to what information will be available online and to whom it will be available will have to be formulated and promulgated. Measures to protect the privacy and integrity of sensitive information will have to be devised, tested, and implemented. New information architectures may be required to support automatic responses to e-mail inquiries. The availability and advantages of e-mail transactions will have to be communicated to citizens. In some cases, agency work processes may have to be re-engineered, staffs reduced, or new talents added to staffs. Special efforts may have to be made to allow access to electronic government services by citizens who are not regular users of the Internet. (We deal below with some of these issues in more detail.) Individuals may need to learn how to access new on-line government services; they may also have to go to the trouble and expense of establishing and learning to use electronic identifiers that will protect the privacy of their communications. In some—perhaps most—cases, these costs will be substantial and will have to be factored into complete cost-benefit analyses of specific e-mail applications. The potential reductions in operating costs identified in our case studies should, therefore, be viewed as upper bounds. Net savings—net of these one-time investment costs—will, of course, be less.

Increased use of e-mail could lower the costs of specific kinds of communication—MSNs, for example, or continued claims for UI benefits. Increased use of e-mail may not, however, bring reductions in agencies' total communications budgets. If e-mail makes some kinds of communication easier, cheaper, or more convenient, the result may be an increase in communication accompanied by a need for additional agency staff to deal with it. If citizens can query government officials by e-mail, they may generate more queries. (The increasing ease and reduced cost of air travel, after all, has not brought a reduction in the total amount spent on air travel.)

Increases in total communications budgets that come about because communication becomes cheaper and easier are not necessarily a bad thing. Indeed, more communication between citizens and governments is probably a good thing, even if it imposes extra costs. Nonetheless, agencies must be prepared to cope with increased costs that may arise because of easier communication. The risk of incurring increased costs may be minimized by concentrating, at least initially, on applications of e-mail to types of communication whose volume is naturally limited or determined by factors unrelated to the medium through which the communication is accomplished. MSNs and continued claims for UI benefits are obvious examples; tax returns and estimates of Social Security benefits are others. Opening channels for citizen-initiated inquiries, however, may generate sharply increased volumes of communication. Allowing e-mail inquiries is probably a laudable goal for the future, but it would probably also be an imprudent first step for government agencies trying to make greater use of e-mail. Better to start with applications that are likely to result in overall budget reductions.

Security

The most difficult operational problem, of course, concerns security: guaranteeing the integrity, authenticity, nonrepudiation, and confidentiality of sensitive e-mail communications. We discuss the issues surrounding security at some length in Chapter Five. It will suffice here to point out that there appear to be no serious technical barriers to providing even very high levels of security. The difficult issues relate to the levels of security that are appropriate to specific kinds of government-citizen communication and the mechanisms through which these levels of security should be provided.

Different government agencies, of course, have different requirements for security. For some purposes, neither encryption of transmitted data nor special steps to certify the identity of sender or receiver may be required. In other applications, the sorts of privacy and integrity protection that are built into many Web browsers—secure sockets layer (SSL) or a secure protocol for multimode e-mail attachments—may be adequate. But it is hard to avoid the conclusion that some potentially very high-volume government e-mail applications will require the level of authentication and user identification afforded only by public key encryption (PKE). Consider:

- Current thinking at HCFA is that positive identification of the recipient will be required before sensitive medical information can be transmitted electronically. Simply sending information to a password-protected e-mail in-box is not seen today as adequate security, since multiple individuals (family members, coworkers, systems administrators, etc.) may have access to that in-box. The required degree of identification security can be provided today only through a PKE system.

- A scheme that made Social Security information available on-line was recently withdrawn after sharp protests, even though on-line access required precisely the same personal information required to retrieve the identical information in a personal visit to a Social Security Administration (SSA) office. Apparently, stronger privacy protection, including a more robust method for establishing the inquirer's identity, will be required if this kind of service is to be accepted by the public.

- Electronic filings of claims for unemployment benefits must be legally binding. Authorities must be able to prosecute someone who files a false claim. Consequently, each claim must include a legally binding nonrepudiatable signature, and today a binding electronic signature can be generated only within a PKE environment.

- The e-mail application that may offer the most dramatic benefits is tax filing. The volume of individualized tax-related communications is immense. Tax returns are complex, and the automatic transcription, processing, and checking facilitated by electronic filing can save both taxpayers and tax collectors considerable time and effort. But, of course, tax returns require binding signatures. Today, electronic federal tax filings require signed paper verification. Presumably, a PKE system will be required to permit fully electronic filing.

We do not mean to suggest that transactions involving nonsensitive data or not requiring positive identification of individual citizens or legally binding electronic signatures should be forced to make use of very secure PKE protocols. We do suggest, however, that e-mail transmission could be of great value in a number of government applications that do require high levels of security, and that at least a few key government agencies should begin to consider how the infrastructure for a national PKE system might be built.[1]

If a national PKE system is required—and we believe that it will be—some attention must be given to what organizations or institutions may appropriately serve as certificate authorities (CAs). Some governmental or quasi-governmental entities have both the local presence and routine contact with individual citizens necessary to serve as CAs. The U.S. Postal Service (USPS), SSA, and state departments

---

[1]Such work is already under way within the Federal Public Key Infrastructure Steering Committee. Public key infrastructure (PKI) initiatives are also under way at the Internal Revenue Service and the Department of Defense.

of motor vehicles are perhaps the most likely candidates. But there is no compelling reason why private-sector firms should not offer CA services alongside or in place of government agencies. Indeed, there is much to recommend a system of multiple CAs, each meeting minimum standards for establishing electronic identities but competing with each other on the basis of price and customer service. Whoever eventually provides CA services, the principal responsibility of government agencies that seek to use e-mail for transmission of sensitive or legally binding information will be to work with other government agencies and private-sector users of PKE systems to promulgate standards for authenticating identities. The aim should be to devise a standard that will satisfy the needs of many users, thereby simplifying and encouraging widespread utilization of secure e-mail facilities.

Free-Form E-Mail

E-mail can provide many advantages when messages are transmitted in a standardized, or predetermined, structure or format. (This would be the case, for example, when citizens fill out and submit Web-based forms.) Our case study of the Medicare program suggests, however, that unstructured, or free-form, e-mail—i.e., correspondence from citizens that is not in a standardized or predetermined format—offers few advantages over telephone or traditional written communication. Indeed, within HCFA, there was an openly articulated fear of growing volumes of unstructured e-mail. In most cases, free-form electronic correspondence cannot be processed automatically: It typically must be read and dealt with by agency personnel in much the same way they deal with other kinds of written correspondence. But because citizens may find it easier to send e-mail than to write a traditional letter, some agency staff fear that the volume of correspondence may grow, increasing the burden on already over-stretched staff. Also, citizens used to very prompt responses to e-mail when communicating with friends or business associates may form unrealistic expectations about the responsiveness of government agencies trying to reply to rising volumes of unformatted e-mail.[2] We also heard concerns that agency staff who have become skilled in responding orally to telephone inquiries may not be as adept in responding in writing to e-mail inquiries. Written responses may have to withstand careful—perhaps even legal—scrutiny, and some fear that if e-mail replaces telephone contacts, useful channels for less-formal communication may be closed.

Information Architectures to Support E-Mail Communication

Another observation that emerges from our case studies is that exploiting the full potential of e-mail may require government agencies to make major investments in information systems—beyond what may be required just to handle e-mail traffic. Part of the attraction of e-mail lies in the opportunities it creates, if it is properly structured or formatted, for at least a degree of automatic processing. Existing data systems, however, may not support such automatic processing. Automatic responses to citizen inquiries or automatic screening of forms for errors or inconsistencies, for example, may require integrated data-banking capabilities that do not exist today. Successful development of HCFA's Medicare Transaction System (MTS) would have been a helpful step toward building a national capability for automated handling of e-mail inquiries relating to Medicare. Cancellation of the MTS initiative and continuation of localized claims processing mean that efforts to move Medicare-related communications via e-mail will have to proceed piecemeal, with individual Medicare contractors offering—or not offering—e-mail communication options to beneficiaries in their service areas. Rather than obtaining information from one or two national centers,

---

[2]Unstructured e-mail offers some advantages, of course, over telephone or traditional written correspondence. It can, for example, be copied, filed, or routed more easily than more traditional communications, and in many cases it can be searched for specific words or content. But even these advantages may be of minimal value if e-mail communication has to be mixed with other forms of communication. The ability to store e-mail in electronic formats may be of little value if the bulk of correspondence handled or stored by an agency is on paper. A system that handles nothing but e-mail correspondence might offer some real advantages, even if the e-mail is unstructured. But for the foreseeable future, government agencies will have to deal with both paper and electronic correspondence, and the ease of handling e-mail may come only at the cost of maintaining separate filing and retrieval systems for different modes of communication.

beneficiaries will have to contact their local carrier or fiscal intermediary. Because Medicare contractors do not all use the same information systems, e-mail options and user interfaces will have to be devised for multiple platforms and data systems. At the California EDD, a centralized database already exists, but significant software upgrades will be required to permit e-mail interactions with existing systems.

Ambitious efforts to develop large new information systems have a way of coming to grief, of course. Reports that such efforts are behind schedule, are over budget, or have been canceled are distressingly common. We do not mean to minimize the difficulty of upgrading existing information systems to take full advantage of e-mail. Neither, however, do we mean to discount the benefits that could arise from greater use of e-mail *without* complex new information systems or major upgrades to existing systems. Even without MTS, for example, it should be possible for Medicare contractors to offer some services on-line. In many cases, the most practical approach will be gradual and will parallel development of improved information systems and e-mail communication options.

However extensive the upgrades to underlying information systems may be, the full costs of these upgrades should not always be associated with the choice to provide citizens with an e-mail channel for communicating with government agencies. Information systems in all government agencies are irregularly upgraded to meet a variety of needs, and the capabilities required simply to support automated processing of e-mail correspondence may turn out to be modest adaptations to upgrades implemented for other reasons. Note, for example, that work on the MTS—a system that would have provided convenient hubs for Medicare-related e-mail communications—was initiated for reasons completely unrelated to e-mail. Similarly, some of the upgrades necessary to support electronic filing of UI claims are already part of EDD's information technology strategic plan. Although some government agencies may not today have the information architecture to exploit e-mail communication, most presumably could build the necessary capabilities into the next generation of information systems—perhaps at modest cost—if e-mail communication with citizens is made part of longer-range information technology planning.

Archives and Audit Trails

Paper has an aura of permanence. Indeed, government agencies are typically required to maintain an archive of the documents flowing to and from them that can be accessed and inspected as needed. One benefit of such an archive is nonrepudiation: If Joan Q. Citizen says she did not send in a form or did not make a formal statement—that is, she repudiates a transaction—retrieval of the relevant document from the archives can prove her wrong. A sequence of such transactions forms an audit trail that can be produced upon demand to provide the context for any individual transaction.

Such paper transactions are almost always human-readable on their face. The set of documents relevant to a transaction is self-descriptive, even years after its origination. Bit strings flung through cyberspace tend not to exhibit these qualities. If Ms. Citizen—after proper authentication—updates her database record at a government agency, does the transaction leave an archived "document" as a trace, or does it just amount to a few bit changes in a database? If her transaction has been encrypted for transmission, should the encrypted version be stored in the agency archives, or should only the unencrypted (plain text) version be saved? If the former, the associated decryption keys will have to be stored indefinitely, which is a major issue. If the latter, will agency personnel or others then be able to perform rapid scans of the data archives to uncover patterns of information that would have been nearly impossible to retrieve from files of paper records? (Large digital archives of transactions are qualitatively different from large paper files; they can be accessed from various terminals—possibly remotely—scanned rapidly for key items of information that can in turn be correlated, and so on.)

Digital archives have another problem: How soon will they become difficult or impossible to access, given rapidly changing computer technology? What logical format and physical medium will survive the generations of hardware and software to be accessible in 10 or 20 years? Rothenberg (1995, p. 24) has investigated these issues and concludes that "digital records . . . are far more fragile than paper." Version 8.0 of a program may no longer be able to read data stored by version 3.5. Modern machines may no longer accept the physical medium.[3] The physical media used for storage also decay at a rather alarming rate: The physical lifetime of media (assuring that no data will be lost) may be as short as one year for magnetic tape, or at most 30 years for a CD-ROM. So just deciding the logical and physical format in which data are to be stored is problematic, and archival storage may require "migrating" the data to new formats and media rather often, and attempting not to lose or change any of the semantic content of those data in the process. How long an archival period is enough?

This report's purpose is not to answer all of these questions. We raise them just to illustrate that as significant volumes of government-citizen communication occur electronically, various agencies will have to address these questions within their own context, most likely with the assistance of agencies such as the National Archives. The issues are technically and administratively solvable, but they do require substantial attention and care.

Managing User Expectations

Many people typically send and receive over 50 e-mail messages a day. When they send a message to a colleague, especially within the United States, they typically expect a response (if not with relevant content, then at least of the automated "I'm on vacation, returning on x/x/xx" variety) often within hours, and almost certainly within a day or two. Persons giving no sign of having received the message after several days might be considered nonresponsive.

Many people also receive near-instantaneous responsiveness from on-line booksellers and other merchants. An electronic order is often followed in minutes by a confirming message, with the physical goods delivered only days later.

However, in sending a letter or form to a government agency, expectations are usually different. For first-class mail, the expectation is three to five days in transit, a week or two to process, and three to five days of return mail transit. Three weeks is not an unreasonable period to await a response.

---

[3]Remember 8-inch floppies? A Control Data Corporation (CDC) model 876 tape reel?

Now consider Joan Q. Citizen sending an e-mail query, or filling out a Web-page form that results in a message, to an agency. What are her expectations? We believe they are more likely to be e-mail-like than postal-mail-like. After all, the agency will probably receive her transmittal seconds after she sends it (by Internet, we assume). Being in machine-readable and -processible form, it can be forwarded to the relevant agency person with the click of a mouse; that person presumably then can access relevant "canned" paragraphs, adding tailored, personalized information as needed, and transmit a response back at near the speed of light.

Would that it were so. Consider this transaction from the agency's viewpoint. Because the agency has offered electronic communication, it receives thousands or tens of thousands of messages a day. Some of them might well be highly formatted ones (e.g., requesting a specific data item from the citizen's on-line record, or changing a data item) that can be handled and responded to entirely automatically. Such transactions will in fact increase the citizen's expectation of immediacy. But other messages will require human thought and intervention and will reside in an in-box of such messages for days or even weeks awaiting processing, just as incoming paper missives might.

The issue, then, is how to manage customers' expectations in an electronic environment. Perhaps a simple rapid response such as the following may suffice: "We have received your message. It appears to require the personal attention of one of our staff members and is currently number 437 in the queue to be processed. We expect to be able to send you an answer within ten working days." Or will the citizen's response be anger that the electronic medium appears to offer little benefit over traditional media and little of the responsiveness that characterizes his or her other e-mail interactions? At a minimum, the managing of customers' expectations needs specific attention from any agency offering substantive, personalized electronic communication to its constituency.

Junk E-Mail and "Spamming"

If the reader has been an active e-mailer, and especially if he or she has interacted with various bulletin boards and forums on the Internet, it is quite certain that he or she has received several messages entitled "Get Rich Quick!!" or "chain letters" offering salvation or other riches. These may be a mild distraction in that they require a mouse-click for deletion.

However, a citizen active in cyberspace may receive a high ratio of junk e-mail to important messages. And if that citizen has "flamed"[4] someone in a message, he or she may even be "spammed."[5,6] (Cyberspace leads to an interesting fluorescence of language, if nothing else!) Several issues arise from such possibilities: (1) The citizen's e-mail in-box may become crammed with unimportant messages, leading him or her to ignore or miss an important communication from a government agency; (2) that e-mail in-box might actually fill up (assuming a fixed amount of space for messages has been allocated by the citizen's ISP), so that a government message may not even be deliverable.

It is also likely that some persons will attempt to imitate official government electronic messages with official-looking message headers and the like, just as junk mail envelopes are periodically received that attempt to look official. There are fewer cues in e-mail than in physical mail to aid the recipient, so unless an unspoofable digital certificate or something similar identifies all-important government messages, this problem will likely recur.

Perhaps even more likely, someone might become angry at a government agency and "spam" that agency's e-mail system so that it becomes clogged and unusable. This situation might be avoided by having the system accept only messages having valid digital certificates attached and perhaps not accept more than two or three mes-

---

[4]*flame* 1. /vi./ To post an email message intended to insult and provoke. 2. /vi./ To speak incessantly and/or rabidly on some relatively uninteresting subject or with a patently ridiculous attitude. 3. /vt./ Either of senses 1 or 2, directed with hostility at a particular person or people. 4. /n./ An instance of flaming.... From *The New Hacker's Dictionary* at http://earthspace.net/jargon/jargon_toc.html.

[5]*spam* /vt.,vi.,n./ [from "Monty Python's Flying Circus"] . . . 2. To cause a newsgroup to be flooded with irrelevant or inappropriate messages . . . 3. To send many identical or nearly-identical messages separately to a large number of Usenet newsgroups. . . . From *The New Hacker's Dictionary* at http://earthspace.net/jargon/jargon_toc.html.

[6]Junk e-mail and spam result in large part from the fact that e-mail is currently very inexpensive, if not free. The sender often incurs no additional cost to send a message to a thousand recipients rather than one. Programming a PC to send a message repetitively hundreds of times a minute may also incur no substantial costs.

sages using the same certificate within some period of time, but even these restrictions could probably be overcome by diligent hackers.

In short, the relatively new medium of e-mail may be abused quite easily, to the point where important communications become lost, ignored, or undeliverable. Legislation dealing with spamming and junk e-mail issues may offer some respite from, and rejoinders to, such activities, but it is as yet unclear whether these measures will suffice. Cranor and LaMacchia (1998) provide a discussion of regulatory and other approaches to the spam problem. They conclude with the cautionary note that technical measures may be somewhat—but not totally—effective; that regulatory approaches are likely to cause undesirable side effects; and that junk e-mail may often be indistinguishable from valid, wanted communications from academic communities, social networks, and individuals. In short, the problem may be manageable, but it will remain a source of irritation for those dependent on e-mail for the conduct of important transactions.

REACHING THE "UNWIRED"

Certainly, outreach and education will be key to reaching those currently "unwired." Many citizens—perhaps especially the elderly and the less-educated poor—have yet to be introduced to e-mail and the Internet and the opportunities for information and communication that they offer. Many still need instruction on the basic techniques necessary to use these new media, as well as information on how and where to find suitable terminals and e-mail services and how to take advantage of specific government applications. In the process of explaining their own on-line offerings, government agencies will have a chance to introduce the Internet more generally.

Although access to the Internet and to e-mail is growing rapidly, a majority of Americans are still unwired. As was shown in Chapter Six, access to the Internet and to e-mail today is concentrated among the middle-aged, the well educated, and the relatively well-to-do. These groups are seldom seen, of course, as the suitable targets for special government services. If efforts to allow e-mail communication with government agencies are perceived as principally benefiting already advantaged populations, support for such initiatives may be weak. This will be especially true if e-mail initiatives are seen as diverting funds from other activities that more directly serve the needs of less-advantaged citizens. In our case studies, we heard clear concerns about the acceptability of providing new services to only a portion—and a relatively privileged portion at that—of the total population served by these agencies. Sustainable support for e-mail communication options is likely to require a plausible prospect of significantly expanded, and perhaps close to universal, access to the Internet and to e-mail.

Because e-mail communication with citizens will often prove more cost-effective than other forms of communication, government agencies will presumably find it fruitful to facilitate or encourage wider use of e-mail. To the extent that e-mail can allow improved service, agencies will also incur some obligation to make these improved services available to as wide a range of citizens as possible. Thus, a plausible case can be made for some sort of public support for expanded e-mail access. But what form should this support take?

Expanding Internet Access

Simple access to terminals capable of supporting e-mail communication does not appear to be a serious problem. The principle of free access to public-use terminals—in libraries, schools, government buildings, social service centers, and other public places—is widely accepted. Such access also appears to be fiscally and administratively feasible, since examples of such public-use terminals abound. The hard policy questions have to do not so much with access *to equipment* as with the character and the extent of free or subsidized access *to the Internet.*

If government agencies limit themselves simply to posting information on Web sites, subsidizing or facilitating access is straightforward and probably noncontroversial. Citizens without access to the Web at home or at work can simply go to a public library, say, and access government Web sites through public-use terminals. Libraries can—and do—limit the time any individual may tie up a terminal as a way to afford others an opportunity for free access. Although it may prove more controversial to do so, libraries can also limit "inappropriate" uses of their equipment (viewing pornography, for example) by installing filters that block access to certain sites or that allow access only to the .gov domain.

Things become more complicated, though, if government agencies seek—as we believe they should—to use the full power of the Internet and e-mail by communicating electronically with individual citizens. For this kind of communication, simple access to a public-use terminal will not be sufficient. Citizens will need individual e-mail accounts and addresses. Messages will have to be stored on some server somewhere, and someone will have to bear the costs of providing and maintaining this server. How might governments subsidize access to individualized e-mail accounts?

A Default Internet Service Provider?

One approach might be for a publicly financed "default" ISP to offer free or highly subsidized e-mail accounts to citizens otherwise without access to e-mail. This provider need not, of course, be operated by a government agency; public funds presumably would pay for or subsidize services actually provided by one or more private ISPs.[7] The costs of providing a bare-bones e-mail service are not high—less than a dollar per year for each five-megabyte individual e-mail storage account, according to industry sources.[8] If increased e-mail usage will reduce government operating costs, providing free or highly subsidized e-mail accounts could be a good public investment.

The rub is that a number of private-sector firms are already providing free e-mail access. These firms make money by carrying advertising. The fact that new free e-mail services continue to be established suggests that this is a profitable business, and private entrepreneurs would undoubtedly complain if they were exposed to direct competition from government-sponsored, advertising-free e-mail services. Their complaints would have considerable legitimacy. Why should public funds be spent to provide a service that is already available, undermining in the process the profitability of already established private providers? And what assurance would there be that pub-

---

[7]For an interesting discussion of approaches that have been used to encourage universal access to a variety of social services, see National Research Council, 1998, Section 2.2.

[8]Presentation at RAND by George Spix, Chief Architect, Consumer Platforms Division, Microsoft Corporation, August 21, 1998.

licly funded e-mail would not also cut into the market for more-traditional, fee-for-service Internet access?

Some of these objections might be overcome if eligibility for publicly funded e-mail service were means tested and available only to individuals or households with incomes below some established threshold. (The analogy here is to telephone Lifeline Service—basic service provided at sharply reduced rates to subscribers who meet certain eligibility criteria.) Low-income individuals would be unlikely subscribers to traditional Internet services, and commercial providers of free e-mail services might not view low-income users as the most important segment of their advertising bases. Such an approach, though, would require some mechanism for certifying eligibility. If providing e-mail service costs only about a dollar per user per year, the cost of the certification mechanism could well exceed the cost of the service itself. And one must wonder whether political support could be mustered for another means-tested government benefit. The current trend seems to be in the other direction.

A government-sponsored service might avoid competition with commercial services, of course, if the government service were sufficiently restricted. Users of the public system could be limited, for example, to sending messages to or receiving messages from addresses in the .gov domain. But such limitations would be inconsistent with the broader social purpose—increasing the network benefits that accrue to all e-mail users whenever a new user establishes access. Current users gain no benefit if they cannot communicate with new users.

In short, publicly funded access to Internet services is likely to be problematic on both policy and political grounds.

E-Mail Addresses for All: A New Role for the Postal Service?

A more promising approach to encouraging expanded use of the Internet might be to create a unique e-mail *address* (as opposed to an e-mail *account*) for every resident of or organization in the United States.[9] Some governmental or quasi-governmental body would as-

---

[9]A recommendation along these lines was advanced by Anderson et al. (1995).

sign these e-mail addresses, which, ideally, would take some systematic and easily derived form, perhaps including a combination of personal name and postal address. Directories of these addresses—with some provision for users who desire the privacy of "unlisted" addresses—would be available on-line.

In essence, these publicly assigned, or "standardized," e-mail addresses would serve as a "national" system of e-mail aliases. An individual who maintains an e-mail account at work, at school, or with a commercial ISP would provide the details of this account (by e-mail, undoubtedly) to the agency that assigns the standardized e-mail addresses. Messages sent to that address would be routed automatically to the individual's personal e-mail account. A message sent to the standardized address of an individual who has not registered a personal e-mail address would be printed and delivered via regular postal mail. Individuals with e-mail accounts might be permitted to specify that messages from specified senders be forwarded only by postal mail. For example, an individual who receives most communications electronically might prefer that potentially sensitive communications—those from, say, the Internal Revenue Service—be delivered by postal mail.[10]

Because a system of this sort would be a hybrid of e-mail and postal mail, USPS might be well positioned to serve as the assigner of the standardized e-mail addresses and as the forwarder of correspondence sent to those addresses.[11] At least the skeleton for such a system already exists, in the form of USPS's computerized system for keeping track of forwarding addresses for normal postal mail. At least in concept, this system could be expanded to include both electronic and postal forwarding addresses for all persons or institutions desiring such a service. USPS does, of course, maintain offices in every community of the country, and postal customers are already ac-

---

[10]For 15 years, RAND employees have enjoyed an electronic/hardcopy option for receiving internal e-mail messages. For some of the thinking behind this option, see Anderson et al., 1989. Interestingly, e-mail has now become so widely accepted that this option is about to go away. Users who wish to retain the hardcopy option will have to pay for it.

[11]USPS has, in fact, begun to make a public case for a national system of e-mail addresses and has suggested that it might be a suitable manager of such a system. See U.S. Postal Service, 1998.

customed to filing change-of-address notices whenever they move. Printing hardcopy messages at a post office close to the intended recipient could reduce delivery times even for recipients who do not use e-mail. And correspondence delivered by USPS already enjoys some legal protections that might more easily be extended to e-mail as a part of some hybrid e-mail/postal-mail system.

A "national" system of e-mail addresses could offer some significant advantages for both government agencies and private correspondents. Senders of messages could enjoy the convenience of *sending* e-mail even if the intended recipient is not able *to receive* messages in electronic form. For those with access to the Internet, typing an e-mail message might well become the routine, or "default," mode of correspondence. If a system of national e-mail addresses were an integral part of a mail forwarding mechanism, correspondence could be sent to an unchanging address with high confidence that the message would eventually reach the intended recipient, even if that recipient had moved. Allowing individuals to specify which kinds of communications they wish to receive on-line might go some way toward centralizing the mechanism for allowing citizens to "opt-in" to e-mail delivery of communications from government agencies. The burden on individual agencies of keeping track of the (possibly changing) preferences of millions of citizens would be reduced. And a national system of e-mail addresses, whether administered by USPS or not, could constitute a basis for building a national infrastructure for secure e-mail. Identity certification could be made an (optional) part of the process of establishing an e-mail forwarding address. Perhaps most important, this kind of hybrid e-mail/postal-mail system could be a key element in an incremental strategy for moving in the direction of near-universal access to e-mail. It would provide strong incentives for using e-mail without penalizing anyone who does not want to or is not yet ready to use e-mail.

A national e-mail address system would have some potential drawbacks, too, however. Directory services or easy-to-derive address formats would certainly increase the utility of standardized e-mail addresses. But these could also open the door to increased volumes of electronic junk mail. No effective mechanisms have been found to limit unsolicited postal mail, and one cannot be sanguine that success will be any better with electronic mail. The possibility of linking electronically available directories with other kinds of personal information may also allow marketing campaigns that are more focused and, to some minds, more intrusive or aggressive. Another potential worry is that a system closely linked with postal mail will give priority to nonsecure correspondence, at least initially. This priority may, of course, be quite reasonable from a broad social perspective. Why complicate the launch of a hybrid e-mail/postal-mail system by including provisions for identity certification, encryption, digital signatures, and so on? But, as we have argued, some potentially important government applications of e-mail will require secure transmission. It would be disappointing if an otherwise attractive approach to making communication by e-mail easier for all citizens had the effect of postponing the day when e-mail can be used for sensitive government communications.

If there is merit in a "national" system of e-mail addresses—and we believe there is—some action may be needed in the near term. In particular, it might be prudent to reserve a specific Internet domain—some have suggested the new .us domain—for such use.

GOVERNMENT'S ROLE

Before many more years have passed, e-mail (or something very like it) will almost surely be as common a mode of communication as telephones are today. Just as surely, e-mail communication between government agencies and citizens will be commonplace. There is good reason to expect that increased use of e-mail will make government operations more efficient. This is, of course, good news; but it is probably not the principal factor that will bring about an increasing volume of government-citizen e-mail traffic. Governments will simply have no choice. When citizens are using e-mail for many other purposes, they will also want to use it to communicate with government agencies.

Increased e-mail access and use will come about whether or not government agencies are aggressive in exploiting the opportunities offered by the Internet and the World Wide Web. In anything but an overtly hostile regulatory or legal environment, purely private forces will guarantee the spread of Internet access and use.[12] So we return to the question with which we began this report: Do government agencies have a special role to play in accelerating or otherwise influencing the spread of Internet access?

Government-sponsored research was, of course, instrumental in the development of the technologies and protocols that form the basis for the Internet. But the rapid expansion of the Internet and the Web in recent years has taken place largely without government involvement. Indeed, many would argue that this expansion was possible precisely *because* government involvement was minimal. We would not suggest that governments should attempt in any way to take over, to guide, or to control development of the Net and the Web. Nonetheless, we do believe that some modest actions by government agencies at the federal, state, and local levels can play a useful role in smoothing the path to near-universal access to e-mail. These actions may allow this near-universal access to be realized earlier than might otherwise be the case, and they may somewhat increase the social benefits that can result from this access.

In particular, government agencies can make useful contributions by attending to some matters that may be neglected by the private sector. Helpful governmental initiatives include the following:

1. **Explore opportunities for individualized e-mail communication.** We have argued that an increasing volume of *individualized* communication between government agencies and citizens is inevitable. But many important operational issues have to be resolved before such communication will be easy and productive. How much e-mail should be expected? What educational or outreach efforts will be required to make citizens aware of opportunities to use e-mail? Will e-mail be structured in a predictable way? What formats will prove easiest to use? How will e-mail communications be processed within agencies? What records of e-mail correspondence will be required? What additional information systems or staff training will be required to handle increased volumes of e-mail? What level of security will

---

[12]Indeed, in a number of countries, Internet use is growing *despite* overtly hostile regulatory and legal environments.

be adequate? How can e-mail channels be protected from "spam"? And on and on.

- These operational issues will not be resolved easily or overnight. What works for one agency will not necessarily work for others. Inevitably, some e-mail applications will fail. Although much can be learned from nongovernmental e-mail management and applications and from the experience of other government agencies, each agency will have to experiment with using e-mail for its own purposes. At the very least, then, it seems prudent for government agencies to determine which of their functions might be facilitated by e-mail communication with individual citizens, to think about what operational obstacles such use may face, and to begin to experiment with e-mail in some of the less demanding applications. The aim is for agencies to begin preparing for the day when they will find it necessary to communicate via e-mail.

2. **Articulate security standards for government e-mail communication.** Internet security is the focus of much innovative and highly competitive activity. Techniques and protocols for secure e-mail communication are already being developed in the private sector. The current generation of Web browsers already supports security arrangements that appear to be adequate for many kinds of Internet commerce. Private-sector firms are already offering the identity certifications necessary to support more-secure PKE and digital signatures. The technology to provide any desired degree of security is already available or being developed. In this environment, there seems little need for direct government intervention.

- But which of the emerging approaches to and implementations of Internet security are adequate for particular kinds of government-citizen communication? Some government applications may plausibly require higher levels of security or more-certain identification of correspondents than is the case for common commercial purposes. Even if the necessary technology is available, there is no guarantee that any private firm will recognize an interest in implementing schemes that provide these higher levels of security, especially if no government agency has clearly articulated a requirement for such security.

- This suggests that at least a few key agencies that deal in large volumes of sensitive communications (tax agencies, agencies responsible for government medical programs, welfare agencies, UI programs, and SSA come immediately to mind) should pursue the process of debating and defining how much and what kind of security will be adequate for their purposes. This process is already well under way, sometimes hastened by specific legislative mandates.[13] Ideally, security standards articulated by these key agencies will be functional rather than technical: Agencies will specify the sorts of protections required, but they will leave open the question of how these protections are to be assured. Knowledge that security at a certain level will allow communication with the Internal Revenue Service, Medicare claims processors, or SSA should act as a powerful spur for private firms to develop and market the necessary technologies and services; there should be no need for government agencies to build the security apparatus to support their own communication needs.

- All agencies will not need the same kinds or levels of e-mail security, of course, and routine use of a higher level of security than is required may prove costly or inconvenient. Nonetheless, efforts by some key agencies to articulate their security needs may result in a small number of standards, each of which can be used for multiple types of government and private transactions—certainly a convenience for all users. Citizens will be able, for example, to establish an electronic identity that will allow communication with multiple government agencies and possibly with many nongovernmental correspondents as well. Agencies will undoubtedly have to certify specific security arrangements and certain providers of secure e-mail services as meeting established standards. If multiple agencies can agree on a small number of standards, this certification process will be much simplified and could possibly be turned over to some central (not necessarily governmental) certification body. What may be needed most today is intensified cross-agency consultation on a limited suite of standards and security requirements that may accom-

---

[13]The Kennedy-Kassenbaum legislation of 1996 (P.L. 104-191), for example, required the Secretary of Health and Human Services to establish privacy standards for electronic transmission of health-related information.

modate the authentication, integrity, nonrepudiation, and confidentiality needs of most agencies.

- Government agencies should not, of course, enforce their own standards on nongovernmental users of secure e-mail. If private customers and vendors are satisfied with lower levels of security for various kinds of electronic commerce than the government requires for the transmittal of, say, Medicare information, these customers and vendors should not be forced to adhere to the higher government standards. The potential volume of communications generated by a handful of key government agencies is such, however, that the security requirements of these agencies are likely to become the standards for many types of e-mail interactions. The sooner these standards can be articulated, the sooner providers and other users of secure Internet services can begin implementing and adjusting to them.

3. **Contribute credibility—and perhaps facilities—to an infrastructure for secure e-mail.** We argued in Chapter Five that the technology to support a nationwide system of secure e-mail already exists. What is lacking, we observed, is the administrative infrastructure for such a system. We also argued that it is neither necessary nor obviously desirable for the government to provide this infrastructure.

- Government agencies can, however, contribute to the creation of this infrastructure by monitoring providers of secure e-mail services and certifying that they meet stringent government standards. In the process, these agencies may lend credibility to a decentralized and nongovernmental infrastructure for secure e-mail, thereby expanding the usefulness of Internet access for many other purposes.[14]

- Although direct government management of an administrative infrastructure for secure e-mail is not necessary, some govern-

---

[14]Some government agencies might find it useful to cooperate with private-sector firms in "co-branding" secure Internet facilities. An insurance company, for example, might develop arrangements for secure Internet transactions with its customers that will also allow its customers to make secure inquiries about the status of Medicare claims. Such an arrangement might prove an attractive marketing device for the insurance company and spare HCFA some of the burden of developing or managing its own mechanisms for secure Internet communications.

ment involvement may be helpful. Some governmental and quasi-governmental agencies maintain extensive systems of local facilities to which citizens already go. Some governmental agencies already require or supply certification of identity as part of their routine operations.

- Such agencies could conceivably play a useful role in the administration of a national secure e-mail system, either by providing CA services directly or by allowing private contractors to lease space in their offices. Post offices or departments of motor vehicles, for example, might turn out to be convenient locations for citizens to go to establish electronic identities. Departments of motor vehicles might even agree to share some parts of their databases with private CAs for the purpose of streamlining the process of establishing electronic identities. Most people, after all, will probably convince a CA that they are who they say they are by producing a valid driver's license.

4. **Create a legal environment supportive of secure e-mail.** E-mail is so new and its uses are expanding so rapidly that no one should be surprised at how many questions relating to the legal status of e-mail remain to be resolved. For their own purposes, and for the sake of facilitating wider use of e-mail communication for nongovernmental purposes, governments have an interest in keeping relevant statutes up to date with evolving patterns of e-mail utilization. Three broad types of issues may have to be resolved (or at least clarified) before e-mail can be easily and widely used for sensitive communications:

- **Allowable encryption.** It is not our intent to enter substantively into the complex and sometimes emotional debates over what kinds of encryption technologies will be permitted for U.S. domestic use or international export, or over what provisions are appropriate for ensuring that authorized law-enforcement personnel can read encrypted e-mail. It suffices to say here that continuing uncertainty over these matters may be retarding the development of useful systems for communicating sensitive information via e-mail. Relevant government agencies can make a significant contribution by working to resolve these issues at the earliest possible date.

- **Standardized digital signatures.** A number of states have enacted legislation establishing criteria for legally binding digital signatures. This interest in supporting increased use of e-mail for legally important documents is, of course, welcome. Unfortunately, these state statutes are not entirely consistent with each other, and today there is some uncertainty associated with using digital signatures for interstate transactions. Greater efforts by state governments to adopt uniform standards, perhaps aided by relevant agencies of the federal government in an advisory capacity, could increase the utility of e-mail for transmission of legally binding documents. Also useful would be consistent standards for the responsibilities of CAs for verifying identities and protecting identity keys.

- **Privacy protection for e-mail.** E-mail today does not enjoy the protections against interception and tampering that are afforded to postal mail and telephone communications. Clearly, e-mail poses some new privacy issues, and postal and telephone protections cannot be transferred directly. Nonetheless, it is difficult to see how e-mail can become a trusted medium for transmitting sensitive information if some sanctions against unauthorized access to or tampering with e-mail are not enacted.

5. **Give special attention to the needs of the "unwired."** We have argued that support for e-mail delivery of government services will be more sustainable if all citizens enjoy access to e-mail, at least at some rudimentary level. For their own purposes and in the interest of social inclusion, government agencies have a special obligation to encourage and support access for the "digitally disadvantaged." There can be little confidence that purely private interests will soon provide Internet access to the poor or the poorly educated. Such provision will have to be a government responsibility. Practically, government encouragement and support may take the form of establishing public-use terminals (with some level of instruction and assistance for would-be users) in locations accessible to citizens who may not have access to the Internet at home, work, or school. Government agencies may also assist some of the "unwired" by providing or subsidizing e-mail accounts. Considerable creativity may be required, however, to devise approaches to providing these subsi-

dies without undermining the private Internet industry that has to date been so successful in expanding e-mail access and use.

6. **Provide e-mail addresses for all.** Earlier in this chapter, we noted that direct government provision of Internet services could prove problematic. Establishing a national system of e-mail addresses coupled with a mail forwarding service—electronically for those with e-mail service and in hardcopy for those without e-mail service—for all citizens who desire it could be a cost-effective approach to expanding communication options for all citizens and for encouraging increased use of e-mail.

ADDITIONAL INFORMATION ON CITIZENS, COMPUTERS, AND CONNECTIVITY

This appendix contains additional information related to Chapter Six. It consists of three parts. First, we explain the procedure for computing "net" differences in home computer access and network service use, and we present a table with "gross" and "net" differences. Second, we explain our approach to statistical tests of the significance of widening or narrowing of gaps between 1993 and 1997. Third, we present additional material, not discussed in Chapter Six, on the purposes for which individuals use home computers.

NET DISPARITIES ACROSS SOCIOECONOMIC GROUPS

The focus of Chapter Six is on disparities across socioeconomic groups in their access to a home computer and their use of network services. As briefly outlined in the main text, tabulations based on raw data may lead to misleading conclusions. For example, in order to assess the impact of income on the diffusion of computers, it would be misleading only to look at disparities across income groups. Part of the gap between low- and high-income families may stem from other socioeconomic characteristics, such as educational attainment. To account for the effects of all other predictor variables of interest, we employ a multivariate regression technique. The six characteristics of interest are household income, educational attainment, race and ethnicity, age, sex, and location of residence (urban or rural).

Both outcome variables, presence of a home computer and use of network services, are binary (yes/no) variables. The use of linear regression techniques, such as ordinary least squares (OLS) or analysis of variance (ANOVA), would be inappropriate, since these do not guarantee that predicted fractions are between 0 and 1. The statistical models most commonly used to estimate binary outcomes are the logistical regression (logit) and probit models. The choice between them is largely arbitrary; we opted for the logit model (Maddala, 1983).

The procedure is as follows. First, we estimate multivariate logit models to explain, say, the presence of a home computer using the six categorical predictor variables listed above. Second, to determine net disparities by, say, sex, for each individual in the sample, we predict the probability that he or she has a home computer under the counterfactual assumption that everyone is female. That is, if everyone were female, but otherwise with the same characteristics that he or she actually has, what would be the probability that each person would have a computer? Third, we average these predicted probabilities over all individuals in the sample to obtain the predicted fraction of the population that would have a computer if everyone were female. This prediction is repeated under the counterfactual assumption that everyone is male, and averaged over all individuals in the sample to obtain an estimate of the fraction having a computer among males. The resulting fractions are termed *net* fractions, as they represent differences that are due only to sex, controlling for all other socioeconomic characteristics of interest. This procedure is repeated for the other five socioeconomic predictor variables. The same procedure is used to compute net percentages of network service users.

Table A.1 shows logit coefficient estimates of 1997 presence of a home computer (column 1) and network service use (column 3). (Columns 2 and 4 are explained below.) Positive values indicate a greater propensity to have a home computer or make use of network services. The omitted category is a non-Hispanic white male age 20 to 39 who lives in a rural area and is a high school graduate (but not a college graduate) with a household income in the bottom quartile. Note that most coefficients are highly significant, in part because of the very large sample sizes (143,129 individuals in 1993 plus 123,249 in 1997).

Table A.1

Logit Estimates

	Access to Home Computer		Use of Network Services	
	1997	1993 – 1997	1997	1993 – 1997
Constant	−1.4651 ***	−1.0032 ***	−1.9056 ***	−0.8034 ***
	(0.0258)	(0.0388)	(0.0337)	(0.561)
Second income quartile	0.7279 ***	0.0055	0.5678 ***	0.2075 ***
	(0.0224)	(0.351)	(0.0315)	(0.531)
Third income quartile	1.4398 ***	−0.1316 ***	1.0508 ***	0.0693
	(0.0213)	(0.0331)	(0.0291)	(0.0500)
Top income quartile	2.2376 ***	−0.0826 *	1.6499 ***	−0.0722
	(0.0230)	(0.0341)	(0.0290)	(0.0495)
Income not reported	0.7223 ***	0.3332 ***	0.6726 ***	−0.2225 ***
	(0.0264)	(0.0429)	(0.0353)	(0.0665)
Enrolled in school	0.1532 ***	0.0925 *	−0.5237 ***	−0.6403 ***
	(0.0326)	(0.0464)	(0.0367)	(0.0777)
High school dropout	−0.5159 ***	0.0602	−1.0167 ***	−0.8207 ***
	(0.0268)	(0.0409)	(0.0413)	(0.0812)
College graduate	0.7375 ***	0.0309	1.1568 ***	−0.3008 ***
	(0.0190)	(0.0261)	(0.0192)	(0.0279)
Hispanic	−0.8745 ***	0.0941 *	−0.7029 ***	0.2389 ***
	(0.0244)	(0.0392)	(0.0329)	(0.0572)
Black	−0.9630 ***	0.2622 ***	−0.6912 ***	0.3851 ***
	(0.0231)	(0.0344)	(0.0298)	(0.0468)
Native American	−0.1609 *	−0.4800 ***	−0.3111 **	0.2625
	(0.0731)	(0.1333)	(0.0981)	(0.1767)
Asian	0.1654 ***	−0.0435	−0.3030 ***	−0.2870 ***
	(0.0344)	(0.0494)	(0.0394)	(0.0722)
Age 0–19	0.2872 ***	−0.0928 *	−0.7096 ***	−1.1899 ***
	(0.0316)	(0.0452)	(0.0364)	(0.0836)
Age 40–59	0.0104	0.0311	−0.2907 ***	0.1931 ***
	(0.0177)	(0.0249)	(0.0189)	(0.0275)
Age 60+	−1.0046 ***	0.0873 *	−1.7937 ***	0.2419 ***
	(0.0234)	(0.0349)	(0.0323)	(0.0512)
Female	0.0018	−0.0065	−0.0809 ***	0.0536 *
	(0.0133)	(0.0188)	(0.0156)	(0.0245)
Urban	0.2179 ***	0.1028 ***	0.4269 ***	−0.1379 ***
	(0.0178)	(0.0254)	(0.0225)	(0.0347)
Location missing	0.1984 ***	0.1107 ***	0.3824 **	−0.1056 *
	(0.0236)	(0.0325)	(0.0286)	(0.0433)

NOTES: Standard errors in parentheses. Significance: * = 5 percent; ** = 1 percent; *** = 0.1 percent.

We estimated similar logit equations for access to a home computer and use of network services at home or work for 1989 and 1993 and computed net rates, as explained above. For each set of predictor variables, Table A.2 shows gross and net rates of home computer penetration and use of network services.

DID DISPARITIES BECOME SMALLER OR LARGER BETWEEN 1993 AND 1997?

We want to determine whether the gaps between socioeconomic groups have widened or narrowed from 1993 to 1997. There are several alternative approaches. For example, we could measure the gap in home computer penetration as the percentage point penetration difference between two groups. For individuals in the lowest and highest income quartiles, 1993 home computer penetration was 7 and 55 percent, respectively, i.e., the gap was 48 percentage points. By 1997, these figures had risen to 15 and 75 percent, respectively, yielding a gap of 60 percentage points. According to this definition, the gap has widened. Alternatively, we could measure the gap as the duration necessary for the disadvantaged group to achieve the penetration level of the advantaged group. Let's explore this definition further.

Figure A.1 shows a stylized home computer penetration model. The penetration rate of new technologies tends to follow a logistic pattern, and we assume that home computers and network use are no exception. Any individual jumps discretely from 0 (no home computer) to 1 (home computer), but population groups as a whole tend to move along the curve from zero penetration to some asymptote, which may or may not be 100 percent. Consider individuals in the lowest income quartile who move from 7 percent in 1993 ($Q1_{93}$) to 15 percent in 1997 ($Q1_{97}$), while those in the top quartile move from 55 percent ($Q4_{93}$) to 75 percent ($Q4_{97}$). During the same time period, the percentage point gap grew from 48 to 60 percent, but did the gap really widen? The growth rate in the lower part of the curve is lower than just above the center, so equal-paced movement to the right implies a widening percentage point differential. If equal-paced growth continues, though, the shape of the curve ensures that the penetration rates will converge.

Table A.2
Gross and Net Percentages of People Who Have Access to a Home Computer and Use Network Services at Home or Work

| | Home Computer | | | | | | Network Services | | | | | |
| | 1989 | | 1993 | | 1997 | | 1989 | | 1993 | | 1997 | |
	Gross	Net	Gross	Net	Gross	Net	Gross	Net	Gross	Net	Gross	Net
Household income												
Bottom quartile	5.7	7.6	7.4	10.1	15.4	20.7	1.7	3.1	2.7	4.7	7.0	11.4
Second quartile	9.3	10.6	16.6	18.5	31.5	33.9	3.4	4.1	7.8	9.1	15.4	17.4
Third quartile	18.0	17.1	30.2	28.0	52.8	49.4	6.4	5.9	13.3	11.9	26.5	24.1
Top quartile	35.0	28.7	54.8	45.9	75.1	66.5	11.5	8.1	23.0	16.6	44.5	34.2
Educational attainment												
High school dropout	6.1	11.4	8.9	17.4	17.2	30.7	0.5	0.8	1.2	2.0	5.3	9.8
High school graduate	14.3	16.1	22.2	23.8	37.3	40.1	6.7	5.7	13.6	10.6	22.7	21.6
College graduate	31.9	26.5	48.7	37.3	65.7	54.5	18.3	11.4	33.8	20.2	55.8	42.4
Race and ethnicity												
Hispanic	7.7	10.3	12.4	17.3	21.8	30.0	2.4	4.2	4.8	8.4	10.0	15.8
Non-Hispanic white	20.2	19.1	30.6	28.8	48.7	46.2	6.9	6.3	13.1	11.9	26.6	24.6
Non-Hispanic black	8.2	11.1	13.3	18.3	22.0	28.5	2.9	4.3	6.3	9.5	11.8	15.9
Native American	7.5	10.5	12.9	19.1	35.3	43.0	2.8	4.8	7.5	11.5	14.0	20.4
Asian	24.1	20.0	37.4	30.9	55.9	49.4	5.2	4.1	9.7	7.6	25.6	20.5
Age category												
0-19	21.5	23.5	30.7	30.6	47.8	48.8	0.6	2.3	1.0	2.9	11.4	19.1
20-39	17.5	16.2	27.6	27.4	43.4	43.3	10.7	7.7	18.6	14.7	33.3	29.6
40-59	22.1	18.5	32.7	28.0	49.3	43.5	9.8	6.6	20.1	13.6	33.2	25.0
60+	5.5	7.7	10.5	14.7	19.7	25.6	0.9	1.1	3.5	4.0	7.4	8.6
Sex												
Male	18.9	18.1	27.9	26.9	43.7	42.4	6.4	6.1	11.8	11.5	24.0	23.3
Female	16.6	17.3	25.9	26.8	41.2	42.5	5.5	5.8	10.9	11.2	21.6	22.2
Location of residence												
Rural	13.2	15.5	19.3	22.9	34.9	39.3	3.9	4.9	7.6	9.5	15.0	18.4
Urban	19.0	18.1	29.2	27.8	44.5	43.3	6.5	6.1	12.5	11.8	25.0	23.8

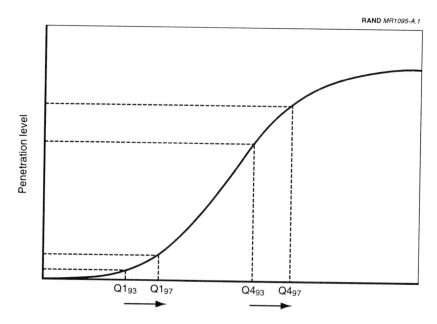

RAND *MR1095-A.1*

Figure A.1—Stylized Home Computer Penetration Between 1993 and 1997, by Income Quartile

Our multivariate logit models follow this penetration model. Column 1 of Table A.1 indicates that the 1997 logit-propensity to have a home computer of the top quartile exceeds that of the bottom quartile (omitted category) by 2.2376, i.e., the horizontal distance between $Q4_{97}$ and $Q1_{97}$ is 2.2376; it is significantly different from zero at 0.1 percent. We estimated the same model using 1993 data; the estimates in column 2 are the difference between 1993 and 1997 coefficient estimates.[1] In other words, estimates for 1993 are the sum of columns 1 and 2. The propensity to have a home computer in 1993 was 2.2376 – 0.0826 = 2.1550 larger for the top income quartile than for the bottom. We present the 1993 incremental (marginal) coefficients, rather than the actual coefficients, because doing so enables us to determine whether the change in the relative propensity was significant. For both home computer presence and use of network

---

[1]To be precise, we estimated both columns simultaneously on pooled 1993 and 1997 data, where column 1 coefficients applied to all data and column 2 to 1993 data only.

services, we find that the gap widened between 1993 and 1997. The wider gap for access to a home computer is significant at 5 percent; the increased gap for use of network services was insignificant. In either case, the gap did not widen substantially.

One way to interpret the horizontal axis is in terms of the period by which one group lags another. Note that the change in the Constant coefficient of column 2 is –1.0032, i.e., the population as a whole moved 1.0032 units to the right between 1993 and 1997. This corresponds to the population-weighted average distance between groups' positions in 1993 and 1997, i.e., the average of $Q1_{97} - Q1_{93}$, $Q4_{97} - Q4_{93}$, and so on for the other quartiles. If the population keeps moving to the right at 1.0032 units every four years, the 1993 bottom quartile may be said to lag behind the top quartile by (1997 – 1993)*2.1550/1.0032 = 8.6 years; by 1997, this lag had increased to 8.9 years. The time gap in use of network services is much shorter: At the rate of adoption experienced between 1993 and 1997, the bottom income quartile may be expected to achieve usage rates equal to those of the top income quartile in just 2.1 years. Thus interpreted, the coefficient estimates in Table A.1, columns 2 and 4, are direct measures of narrowing or widening of gaps. Table 6.1, in the concluding section of Chapter Six, summarizes changes in gaps from 1993 to 1997 using these data. Only differences that are significant at a 5 percent confidence level or better are recorded as changes.

THE USE OF HOME COMPUTERS

We conclude with extensive tabulations of various dimensions of home computer access and use. For individuals with a home computer, Table A.3 shows the average age of the (newest) computer in years. Overall, the stock of home computers in the United States is, on average, just two years and three months old. About one out of four computerized households has more than one computer. For each individual age 3 or older living in a household with a computer, the CPS asks whether that individual uses the computer directly. Overall, 71.2 percent of those with a home computer use the computer directly.

Table A.3

Computer Use at Home

	Among Those with a Home Computer			Among Those That Directly Use the Home Computer												
	Est. ave. age of newest comp. (yrs)	Have more than one comp. in household	Use comp. for any purpose	Word process.	Book-keep., finance, taxes, household records	E-mail	Desktop pub., news-letters	Games	Graphic design	Data-bases	Spread-sheets	Internet, other on-line service	Connect to comp. at work or school	Work at home	School assignments	Learning to use comp.	Use comp. 5+ days per week
Total	2.24	24.8	71.2	60.9	40.0	35.9	16.7	62.8	23.4	24.2	26.5	42.1	10.2	31.7	30.1	20.0	33.4
Sex																	
Male	2.19	26.2	72.0	57.0	42.3	39.1	16.3	66.4	24.0	27.4	30.2	47.9	12.9	35.0	28.5	19.3	37.7
Female	2.22	24.2	70.3	64.9	37.3	33.9	17.1	58.5	22.8	21.2	23.1	38.0	8.3	28.2	31.3	20.3	29.9
Age category																	
0-19	2.13	24.8	71.6	41.6	5.6	20.5	8.9	81.0	18.4	9.3	9.4	34.7	2.7	7.1	57.3	23.6	29.3
20-29	2.02	22.6	75.8	71.3	35.1	47.9	16.3	59.6	24.0	23.0	26.4	48.3	17.2	26.4	36.1	17.5	38.6
30-39	2.11	23.8	76.3	68.7	48.3	45.7	19.3	58.3	27.7	27.0	31.1	45.6	15.8	39.2	13.3	18.9	35.0
40-49	2.25	28.9	72.1	71.4	46.5	43.9	18.9	50.4	27.3	28.0	30.8	44.3	14.9	39.2	12.2	17.4	34.7
50-59	2.45	28.1	65.7	73.4	48.2	44.3	18.0	43.7	25.8	30.3	30.7	42.5	13.5	41.2	8.3	17.3	36.6
60+	2.82	21.4	54.1	68.1	49.3	36.5	13.4	46.4	20.8	24.3	24.1	33.9	5.4	22.8	3.1	17.7	39.1
Education																	
< High school	2.19	23.2	69.2	58.0	8.9	25.9	8.1	69.7	19.7	8.5	8.5	31.5	3.3	7.8	65.4	17.4	34.7
HS graduate	2.23	21.4	66.7	65.5	40.3	39.0	15.0	58.3	25.0	22.1	23.9	39.8	10.7	25.8	20.9	19.0	34.1
College grad.	2.25	31.2	82.5	79.0	49.1	52.8	21.6	46.4	27.4	32.4	36.2	51.1	20.4	47.0	15.1	16.0	39.6

Table A.3 (continued)

	Among Those with a Home Computer			Among Those That Directly Use the Home Computer													
	Est. ave. age of newest comp. (yrs)	Have more than one comp. in household	Use comp. for any purpose	Word process.	Book-keep., finance, taxes, household records	E-mail	Desktop pub. newsletters	Games	Graphic design	Data-bases	Spread-sheets	Internet, other on-line service	Connect to comp. at work or school	Work at home	School assignments	Learning to use comp.	Use comp. 5+ days per week
Race/ethnicity																	
Hispanic	1.89	17.8	61.5	55.8	33.8	27.8	14.5	59.6	20.1	19.9	20.3	38.0	7.5	27.7	34.6	23.5	32.1
White	2.23	25.9	72.7	61.7	40.6	37.9	17.1	62.9	24.0	24.8	27.2	43.9	10.9	32.0	28.9	19.4	34.1
Black	2.13	17.5	66.5	55.6	38.7	27.0	15.1	62.5	20.5	21.0	24.6	33.7	8.8	31.0	32.9	20.9	31.2
Native Amer.	2.27	24.0	61.5	54.4	36.0	30.2	19.8	66.6	31.1	29.0	25.5	36.2	9.5	30.8	33.9	20.7	38.9
Asian	2.15	30.7	63.7	59.8	32.6	36.0	12.8	58.0	19.9	23.4	26.5	44.5	12.0	30.3	38.9	22.0	35.9
Location																	
Rural	2.34	17.7	69.6	56.0	40.1	27.6	15.4	67.5	23.5	21.1	23.0	33.8	6.5	27.0	30.2	18.1	31.4
Urban	2.16	27.1	71.3	61.8	39.9	38.5	17.0	61.5	23.5	25.2	27.7	45.1	11.7	33.6	29.4	20.5	34.7
income quartile																	
Bottom	2.13	18.7	66.5	58.8	31.7	33.5	12.8	62.8	22.2	19.4	21.6	38.2	9.7	20.0	35.9	22.1	36.6
Second	2.23	15.3	67.8	56.4	37.6	30.2	15.6	66.7	22.6	20.4	20.8	36.7	7.0	24.7	30.9	22.5	33.4
Third	2.29	20.8	70.3	57.3	40.1	33.3	16.3	65.4	23.6	23.4	25.0	40.1	8.6	29.4	28.9	20.3	32.0
Top	2.13	33.4	74.8	65.9	42.4	42.5	18.3	60.2	24.2	28.1	31.6	49.7	14.0	39.0	29.5	18.8	34.3
Employment status																	
Student	2.12	25.5	70.8	43.4	9.1	22.4	10.1	79.2	18.5	13.2	14.9	38.8	4.8	9.8	58.7	23.5	29.9
Employee	2.22	24.3	73.8	70.8	44.9	45.0	17.8	55.4	26.6	26.8	30.5	45.0	15.8	38.0	14.6	17.5	33.5
Employer	2.20	33.7	72.4	68.4	57.3	46.9	23.6	45.0	28.9	34.4	34.0	47.8	15.0	56.8	8.1	17.2	46.5
Unemployed	2.12	24.1	74.8	69.4	37.1	41.3	17.5	56.4	27.4	24.0	27.3	44.6	6.4	17.1	21.2	26.3	43.5
Other	2.36	22.7	62.3	64.8	34.5	35.9	13.1	56.6	20.6	17.3	17.1	35.7	4.6	10.6	24.8	19.2	37.2

Table A.3 (continued)

	Among Those with a Home Computer			Among Those That Directly Use the Home Computer													
	Est. ave. age of newest comp. (yrs)	Have more than one comp. in house-hold	Use comp. for any purpose	Word process.	Book-keep., finance, taxes, house-hold records	E-mail	Desktop pub., news-letters	Games	Graphic design	Data-bases	Spread-sheets	Inter-net, other on-line service	Connect to comp. at work or school	Work at home	School assign-ments	Learn-ing to use comp.	Use comp. 5+ days per week
School type																	
Public HS	2.23	23.3	88.2	60.8	3.6	25.8	8.0	71.9	20.5	7.0	7.6	30.9	2.6	5.7	79.3	18.5	35.0
Private HS	2.16	35.1	92.1	72.5	3.1	35.3	10.8	70.1	24.8	9.7	9.0	40.6	6.3	10.1	85.2	19.5	42.6
Public college	2.09	27.1	82.9	81.5	26.1	48.3	16.3	53.1	26.9	24.1	27.2	47.3	21.2	22.5	80.0	20.2	43.5
Private college	2.04	35.2	75.7	82.9	27.2	56.6	19.9	47.5	28.5	29.7	28.7	53.9	29.7	29.8	79.5	19.4	46.5
Disability status																	
Able	2.20	25.3	71.5	60.8	39.9	36.6	16.8	62.6	23.5	24.5	26.9	43.3	10.7	31.9	30.2	19.8	33.9
Disabled	2.31	22.8	57.9	64.9	36.0	33.2	12.4	58.1	22.8	19.5	19.6	34.5	7.9	22.9	13.8	20.3	34.8
Region																	
Northeast	2.26	23.3	69.6	58.5	36.6	36.2	14.9	60.1	20.5	23.0	23.2	43.9	10.2	30.8	29.9	20.3	32.7
Midwest	2.24	23.6	71.6	59.3	39.8	34.1	16.4	65.1	23.3	23.7	26.9	41.0	10.4	30.8	31.0	19.9	30.8
South	2.15	25.0	71.5	59.5	41.0	36.8	15.9	63.3	22.6	24.0	26.5	43.6	10.4	31.6	28.0	17.4	35.7
West	2.19	28.4	71.5	65.8	40.8	39.0	19.1	61.0	26.8	26.4	29.4	43.7	11.5	33.3	31.2	22.2	35.5

For those who use a computer at home, the CPS then asks how often and for what purposes the individual uses the computer. The most common use, at 62.8 percent, is to play games, followed closely by word processing. Other popular uses are bookkeeping or keeping track of finances, taxes, or household records; connecting to the Internet; sending e-mail; working at home; and doing school assignments. Home computers appear to be used quite intensively: about one out of three home computer users reports using it at least five days per week. Three out of four use it at least two days per week (not shown in the table).

WHERE TO CONTACT THE GOVERNMENT

The following is a list of national government agency Web addresses. The Web sites contain information on the agencies themselves as well as e-mail addresses for government officials.

LEGISLATIVE BRANCH

U.S. Senate (106th Congress)

http://www.senate.gov/contacting

U.S. House of Representatives (106th Congress)

http://www.house.gov/house/MemberWWW.html

EXECUTIVE BRANCH

The White House, Executive Office of the President (EOP) and Office of the Vice President

http://www.whitehouse.gov/WH/Mail/html/Mail_President.html

http://www.whitehouse.gov/WH/Mail/html/Mail_Vice_President.html

Department of Agriculture (USDA)

http://www.usda.gov/message.htm

Department of Commerce (DOC)

http://www.doc.gov/

Department of Defense

http://www.defenselink.mil/faq/comment.html

Department of Education

http://www.ed.gov/

Department of Energy

http://home.doe.gov/people/peopda.htm

Department of Health and Human Services (HHS)

http://www.hhs.gov/about/contacthhs.html

Department of Housing and Urban Development (HUD)

http://www.hud.gov/assist.html

Department of the Interior (DOI)

http://www.doi.gov/contacts.html

Department of Justice (DOJ)

http://www.usdoj.gov/02organizations/02_1.html

Department of Labor (DOL)

http://www.dol.gov/dol/public/contacts/main.htm

Department of State

http://www.state.gov/www/feedback1.html

Department of Transportation (DOT)

http://www.dot.gov/feedback.htm

Department of the Treasury

http://www.ustreas.gov/opc/opc0005.html

Department of Veterans Affairs

http://www.va.gov/customer/consumer.htm#poc

JUDICIAL BRANCH

U.S. Supreme Court, Circuit Courts, and Courts of Appeal

http://www.uscourts.gov/PubAccess.html

http://www.uscourts.gov/allinks.html#all

http://www.uscourts.gov/contact.html

WEB SITES THAT PROVIDE LINKS TO MANY GOVERNMENT AGENCIES

FedWorld, maintained by the national Technical Information Service of the Department of Commerce

http://www.fedworld.gov/

Government Information Xchange, maintained by the General Services Administration

http://www.info.gov/

REFERENCES

Anderson, Robert H., Tora K. Bikson, Sally Ann Law, and Bridger M. Mitchell (1995). *Universal Access to E-Mail: Feasibility and Societal Implications*, Santa Monica, CA: RAND, MR-650-MF.

Anderson, Robert H., Norman Z. Shapiro, Tora K. Bikson, and Phyllis H. Kantar (1989). *The Design of the MH Mail System*, Santa Monica, CA: RAND, N-3017-IRIS.

The Benton Foundation (1998). "Defining the Technology Gap," *Losing Ground Bit by Bit: Low Income Communities in the Information Age*, Washington, D.C.: The Benton Foundation, pp. 1–8.

Bikson, T. K. (1997). *Roadmap to Electronic Document Management in United Nations Organizations*, Geneva: UN Information Systems Coordination Committee (ISCC), ACC/1997/ISCC/5.

Bikson, T. K. (forthcoming). "Managing Digital Documents: Technology Challenges and Institutional Responses," *Proceedings of the International Conference of the Round Table on Archives*, Stockholm: International Council on Archives.

Bikson, T. K., and J. D. Eveland (1990). "The Interplay of Work Group Structures and Computer Support," in R. Kraut, J. Galegher, and C. Egido (eds.), *Intellectual Teamwork*, Hillsdale, NJ: Erlbaum Associates, pp. 245-290.

Bikson, T. K., and E. Frinking (1993). *Preserving the Present: Toward Viable Electronic Records*, The Hague: Sdu Publishers.

Bikson, T. K., et al. (1991). *Networked Information Technology and the Transition to Retirement: A Field Experiment*, Santa Monica, CA: RAND, R-3690-MF.

California Employment Development Department (1994). "Fact Sheet: Unemployment Insurance Program," Sacramento, CA, DE 8714B, Rev. 11.

California Employment Development Department (1996a). "Fraud Fact Sheet," Sacramento, CA (March).

California Employment Development Department (1996b). "A Guide to Unemployment Insurance Benefits," Sacramento, CA, DE 1275A, Rev. 34.

California Employment Development Department (1996c). "Telecommunication Technology Fact Sheet," Sacramento, CA.

California Employment Development Department (1996d). "Telephone Claim Filing Education and Outreach Fact Sheet," Sacramento, CA.

California Employment Development Department (1996e). "Unemployment Insurance Overview," Sacramento, CA (March).

California Employment Development Department, Information Technology Branch (1996). *Information Technology Strategic Plan*, Sacramento, CA (May).

California Employment Development Department, Project Management Division (1995). "Unemployment Insurance Automated Claim Filing Feasibility Study Report," internal document.

California Employment Development Department, Project Management Division (1996). *Project Management Division Strategic Plan*, Sacramento, CA (September).

Cranford, J. (1995). "A Guide to Award-Winning Technology," *Governing* (January), pp. 61–72.

Cranor, Lorrie Faith, and Brian A. LaMacchia (1998). "Spam!" *Communications of the ACM*, 41(8) (January), pp. 74–83.

Crowston, K., T. W. Malone, and F. Lin (1986). "Cognitive Science and Organizational Design," *Proceedings of the CSCW Conference*, NY: Association for Computing Machinery, pp. 135–144.

De Michelis, G., and M. A. Grasso (1994). "Situating Conversations Within the Language/Action Perspective: The Milan Conversation Model," *Proceedings of the CSCW Conference*, NY: Association for Computing Machinery, pp. 89–100.

Educational Testing Service (1997). *Computers and Classrooms: The Status of Technology in U.S. Schools*, Princeton, NJ: Educational Testing Service.

Eisenach, J. A. (1997). *The Digital State*, Washington, D.C.: Progress & Freedom Foundation and IBM's Institute for Electronic Government. Also available from Progress & Freedom Foundation at pff@aol.com.

Federal Public Key Infrastructure Steering Committee (1998). "Access with Trust," Washington, D.C.: Office of Management and Budget, Government Information Technology Services Board (September). Also available at http://gits.gov.

Firestone, Charles, and Amy Korzick Garner (1998). Foreword to *Investing in Diversity*, Washington, D.C.: The Aspen Institute, pp. v–xi.

Forsyth, Barbara H., and W. Sherman Edwards (1997). *Market Research on the Information Needs of HCFA Beneficiaries: General Medicare Population Focus Groups*, Westat (September).

Geer, Daniel E., Jr. (1998). "Risk Management Is Where the Money Is," speech to Digital Commerce Society of Boston (November 3). Available at http://catless.ncl.ac.uk/Risks/20.06.html.

Governor's Council on Information Technology (1995). *Getting Results*, Sacramento, CA.

Hochschild, Jennifer L. (1981). *What's Fair: American Beliefs About Distributive Justice*, Boston: Harvard University Press.

Hoffman, D. L., W. Kalsbeek, and T. P. Novak (1996). "Internet and Web Use in the United States: Baseline for Commercial

Development," *Communications of the ACM*, 39(12) (December), pp. 36–46.

Hoffman, D. L., and T. P. Novak (1998). "Bridging the Racial Divide on the Internet," *Science*, 280 (17 April), pp. 390–391.

Hoffman, D. L., T. P. Novak, and Alladi Venkatesh (1998). "Diversity on the Internet: The Relationship of Race to Access and Usage," *Investing in Diversity*, Washington, D.C.: The Aspen Institute.

Information Technology Support Center (1997). *Planning Guidance Document for Telephone Initial Claims*, Version 2.0 (May). Available at http://www.itsc.state.md.us/ITSC/delvrbles/Deliverables/P06/PGD/pgd.html.

Internal Revenue Service (1998). *FY 1996 Cost of Submission Processing in the Service Centers*, Document 10806 (03-98).

Katz, James E., and Philip Aspden (1996). "Motivations for and Barriers to Internet Usage: Results of a National Public Opinion Survey," paper presented at 24th Annual Telecommunications Policy Research Conference, Solomons, MD (October).

Katz, James E., and Philip Aspden (1997a). *Internet Dropouts: The Invisible Group*, Morristown, NJ: Bellcore. Also available on the Markle Foundation Web site: http://www.markle.org.

Katz, James E., and Philip Aspden (1997b). *Motivations for and Barriers to Internet Usage: Results of a National Public Opinion Survey*, Morristown, NJ: Bellcore.

Kennedy School of Government (1993). "Info/California: Where Do Electronic Government Tellers Belong?" Case and Epilogue: C16-93-1204.0 and C16-93-1204.1.

Kraut, Robert, et al. (1996). "The HomeNet Field Trial of Residential Internet Services," *Communications of the ACM*, 39(12) (December), pp. 55–63.

Kreuger, Alan (1993). "How Computers Have Changed the Wage Structure: Evidence from Microdata, 1984–1989," *Quarterly Journal of Economics*, 108, pp. 33–60.

Krieg, Richard (1995). "Information Technology and Low-Income, Inner City Communities," *Journal of Urban Technology*, 3(1), pp. 1–17.

Lai, K. Y., and T. W. Malone (1988). "Object Lens: A 'Spreadsheet' for Cooperative Work," *Proceedings of the CSCW Conference*, NY: Association for Computing Machinery, pp. 115–124.

Macfadden & Associates, Inc. (1996). *Top Issues Survey: Report of Findings*, Silver Spring, MD: Macfadden & Associates.

Maddala, G. S. (1983). *Limited-Dependent and Qualitative Variables in Econometrics*, Cambridge, UK: Cambridge University Press.

Malone, T. W., K. Y. Lai, and C. Fry (1992). "Experiments with Oval: A Radically Tailorable Tool for Cooperative Work," *Proceedings of the CSCW Conference*, NY: Association for Computing Machinery, pp. 289–297.

Mayer-Schönberger, V. (1999). "Tele-Privacy: The European Union Directive on Data Protection in Telecommunications," *Proceedings of the 26th Telecommunications Policy Research Conference*, Washington, D.C..

Medina-Mora, R., T. Winograd, R. Flores, and F. Flores (1992). "The Action Workflow Approach to Workflow Management Technology, *Proceedings of the CSCW Conference*, NY: Association for Computing Machinery, pp. 281–288.

Milward, H. B., and L. O. Snyder (1996). "Electronic Government: Linking Citizens to Public Organizations Through Technology," *Journal of Public Administration Research and Theory*, 6(2), pp. 261–275.

National Partnership for Reinventing Government (1993). *Access America: Reengineering Government Through Information Technology*, Washington, D.C.: U.S. Government Printing Office. Also available at http://www.npr/gov/library/reports/it.html.

National Research Council (1996). *Cryptography's Role in Securing the Information Society*, Washington, D.C.: National Academy Press.

National Research Council (1998). *Fostering Research on the Economic and Social Impacts of Information Technology: Report of a Workshop*, Washington, D.C.: National Academy Press.

National Research Council, Computer Science and Telecommunications Board (1997a). *More Than Screen Deep: Toward Every-Citizen Interfaces to the Nation's Information Infrastructure*, Washington, D.C.: National Academy Press.

National Research Council, Computer Science and Telecommunications Board (1997b). *Fostering Research on the Economic and Social Impacts of Information Technology*, Washington, D.C.: National Academy Press.

National Science Foundation (1998). *Program Announcement: Digital Government*, Washington, D.C.: NSF Directorate for Computer and Information Science and Engineering, NSF98-121 (June). Also available at http://www.nsf.gov/pubs/nsf98121.html.

National Telecommunications and Information Administration (1998). *Falling Through the Net II: New Data on the Digital Divide*, Washington, D.C.: U.S. Government Printing Office.

Neu, C. R., R. H. Anderson, and T. K. Bikson (1998). *E-Mail Communication Between Government and Citizens: Security, Policy Issues, and Next Steps*, Santa Monica, CA: RAND, IP-178. Also available at http://www.rand.org.

Office of Management and Budget, *Budget of the United States Government, Fiscal Year 1999*, Washington, D.C.: U.S. Government Printing Office, 1998.

Office of Technology Assessment (1991). *Rural America at the Crossroads: Networking for the Future*, Washington, D.C.: U.S. Government Printing Office.

Perlman, E. (1994). "The Cyber-lawyer Is In," *Governing* (October), pp. 37–38.

Rothenberg, Jeff (1995). "Ensuring the Longevity of Digital Documents," *Scientific American*, 272(1), pp. 24–29.

San Diego State University, Center for Learning, Instruction and Performance Technologies (1996). *Principles for One-Stop Information and Training: Initial Analysis of Technical Trends and Usability Issues* (May).

Schofield, J. W. (1995). *Computers, Classroom Culture, and Change,* Cambridge, UK: Cambridge University Press.

Schofield, J. W., and A. L. Davidson (1997). "The Internet in School: The Shaping of Use by Organizational, Structural, and Cultural Factors," in S. Lobodzinski and I. Tomek (eds.), *Proceedings of WebNet 97—World Conference of the WWW, Internet & Intranet,* Charlottesville, VA: Association for the Advancement of Computing in Education, pp. 485–489.

Sproull, Lee (in press). "Computers in the U.S. Household: 1977–1997," in Alfred D. Chandler, Jr., and James W. Cortada (eds.), *The Information Age in Historical Perspective: The Role of Information in the Transformation of the United States from Colonial Times to the Present,* New York: Oxford University Press.

Swope, C. (1995). "A Hang-Up for On Line Government," *Governing* (December), pp. 49–50.

U.S. Bureau of the Census (1985). *Current Population Survey,* October 1984, Washington, D. C.: U.S. Bureau of the Census.

U.S. Bureau of the Census (1990). *Current Population Survey,* October 1989, Washington, D.C.: U.S. Bureau of the Census.

U.S. Bureau of the Census (1994). *Current Population Survey,* October 1993, Washington, D.C.: U.S. Bureau of the Census.

U.S. Bureau of the Census (1998). *Current Population Survey,* October 1997, Washington, D.C.: U.S. Bureau of the Census.

U.S. House of Representatives (1997a). *Social Security Administration's Website,* testimony of David C. Williams, inspector general, Social Security Administration, before Subcommittee on Social Security, Committee on Ways and Means, 105th Cong., 1st sess. (May 6), pp. 34–51.

U.S. House of Representatives (1997b). *Social Security Adminis-tration's Website,* testimony of John J. Callahan, acting com-missioner of Social Security, before Subcommittee on Social Security, Committee on Ways and Means, 105th Cong., 1st sess. (May 6), pp. 6–34.

U.S. Postal Service (1998). *Comments on Enhancement of the .us Domain Space,* made before Department of Commerce, Na-tional Telecommunications and Information Administration (October 2). Available at http://www.ntia.doc.gov/ntiahome/domainname/Campbell.htm.

U.S. Senate (1997). *Encryption, Key Recovery, and Privacy Protection in the Information Age,* testimony of Peter Neumann before Senate Committee on the Judiciary, 105th Cong., 1st sess. (July 9), pp. 68–104, 107–121.

Wilhelm, Anthony (1998). *Closing the Digital Divide: Enhancing Hispanic Participation in the Information Age,* Claremont, CA: The Tomas Rivera Policy Institute.

Winograd, T. (1987). "A Language/Action Perspective on the Design of Cooperative Work," *Human Computer Interaction,* 3, pp. 3-30.

Winograd, T., F. Flores, M. Graves, and B. Hartfield (1988). "Com-puter Systems and the Design of Organizational Interaction," *ACM Transactions on Office Information Systems,* 6(2), pp. 153–172.